Privacy and Fame

Privacy and Fame

How We Expose Ourselves Across Media Platforms

Yuval Karniel and Amit Lavie-Dinur

LEXINGTON BOOKS
Lanham • Boulder • New York • London

Published by Lexington Books
An imprint of The Rowman & Littlefield Publishing Group, Inc.
4501 Forbes Boulevard, Suite 200, Lanham, Maryland 20706
www.rowman.com

Unit A, Whitacre Mews, 26-34 Stannary Street, London SE11 4AB

British Library Cataloguing in Publication Information Available

Library of Congress Control Number: 2015952180
ISBN: 978-1-4985-1077-6 (cloth : alk. paper)
eISBN: 978-1-4985-1078-3

∞™ The paper used in this publication meets the minimum requirements of American
National Standard for Information Sciences—Permanence of Paper for Printed Library
Materials, ANSI/NISO Z39.48-1992.

Printed in the United States of America

Contents

Acknowledgments

This book would not have been possible without the professional assistance and support of our editors Alison Pavan and Kasey Beduhn.

We want to give a special thanks to Natali Morad for her dedicated help throughout the years researching and editing the articles that serve as the basis of this book. In addition, we would like to thank our team of researchers: Candice Kotzen, Tom Divon, Keren Goldenzweig, Maayan Yani and Michal Alfassi-Herman for all their hard work. Without their continued efforts we would have not been able to bring this work to a successful completion.

We would like to thank our students for being the first to hear the ideas and findings discussed in the book and to share their thoughts on the matter—they are a constant source of inspiration.

We would like to thank our colleagues at The Sammy Ofer School of Communications at the Interdisciplinary Center (IDC) Herzliya for engaging in lengthy and dynamic discussions with us about the ideas presented in this book. We would like to give a special thanks to the school's Dean, Dr. Noam Lemelshtrich Latar, for providing us the opportunity to work on this book and for his encouragement to pursue this and other projects over the years.

Above all we would like to thank our families for all their encouragement and support.

Chapter 1

Privacy and Popularity

An Introduction

Mark Zuckerberg, the then 25-year-old chief executive officer and founder of Facebook, caused a commotion in a January 2010 interview, when he responded to a question about the future of online privacy by candidly stating that privacy was no longer a "social norm" (Johnson, 2010). According to Zuckerberg, "People have really gotten comfortable not only sharing more information and different kinds, but more openly and with more people. That social norm [with reference to "privacy"] is just something that has evolved over time" (quoted in Sarvas & Frohlich, 2011, p. 165).

Zuckerberg was referring to today's ubiquitous culture of openness and self-exposure in which individuals are increasingly willing to share personal information about themselves, traditionally considered as private, in the public sphere. In just over a decade, individuals have gone from asking "Why should I put any information on the Internet at all" to posting intimate information online. This is reflected in media technologies, which continue to manifest from the norm of "private by default, public through effort" in the direction of "public by default, private through effort." The preceding manifestation accentuates the pathway from Web 1.0 (go search, get data) to Web 2.0 (real identities, real relationships) with a final emergence in Web 3.0 (real identities generating massive amounts of data). This ubiquitous computing era identifies how being watched has become part and parcel of "participating." Indeed, today Facebook has more than 1.44 billion monthly (890 million daily) active users who, each day, share nearly five billion items, upload 350 million photos and click the "like" button more than 4.5 billion times. Additionally, Facebook stores more than 300 petabytes of users data (Smith, 2015).

This leads to an increase in public exposure, invoking the value that liberal society places on openness and the liberal credo of "quantity versus quality of information." Importantly, a new media culture emerges here that values exposure owing to the greater "openness" it fosters. As such, it has become more and more possible for individuals to talk about intimate matters in public. Once these intimate matters are released into the public sphere, they leave their mark there as well as on each individual's conceptualizations and expectations of privacy—blurring the traditional distinctions between the private and public space. Indeed, rapid technological advances in communications, among them Internet access, social networks and the prevalence of mobile phones with cameras, are making it easier than ever before to share and access personal information about ourselves and others (Buchanan, Paine, Joinson, & Reips, 2007; DeCew, 1997, p. 145; Katsh, 1989). The result is that, for most people, it has becoming increasingly difficult to imagine life without the perspective of other people upon them, and accordingly, individuals continue to lose any general sense of the difference made by the possible presence of this perspective (Rossler, 2005, p. 175). Rather than opting out or going off the "grid," many individuals are developing techniques to manage the dynamics of life under a constant state of surveillance (Boyd, 2011). One thing is clear: the traditional notions of privacy are changing.

This book, *Privacy and Fame: How We Expose Ourselves Across Media Platforms*, explores the changing nature of privacy—changes in perceptions, expectations and actual behavior concerning privacy and privacy exposure— to better understand the various ways individuals negotiate the boundaries between the private and public self across different media platforms. This book examines the relationship between both evolving social norms regarding privacy and the emergence of new media technologies, in order to examine how these two forces intensify and perpetuate the erosion of traditional expectations and notions of privacy (Cohen, 2012). Reality TV, social networks, mobile phones and blogs are all founded on the willingness of individuals to share their personal information, their photos, political affinities and locations as well as thoughts and feelings with the general public. It is through an analysis of these mediums, and the application of a unique privacy typology, that the book aims to trace the evolution of the concept of privacy and to examine the different ways individuals engage in privacy exposure. This book does not provide a doomsday scenario of privacy loss nor does it particularly lament this seeming loss of privacy. Rather, the book treats privacy loss as a feature of modern society that needs to be better understood, examined and analyzed.

Current academic and legal discourse describes privacy as something that is essential for the formation of the self, for individual autonomy, for establishment of intimate and personal relationships with others and for maintaining a robust, democratic society (Cohen, 2012; Rosen, 2000; Rossler, 2005). Yet, while academic and legal discourse place a high value on privacy, research and observation reveal a gap between this discourse and the way individuals actually behave in real life (Tufekci, 2008). This behavior reveals increasing levels of privacy exposure and reflects very different notions of privacy, suggesting that privacy is conceptualized by most as a form of social currency to be exchanged for convenience and fame, rather than a value to be protected and guarded. Indeed, recent work in privacy theory asserts the importance of context in structuring privacy expectations and interests (Cohen, 2012, p. 128; Nissenbaum, 2010). Specifically, Helen Nissenbaum's theory of contextual integrity (as expressed in Nissenbaum, 2004) is based on two principles: (1) People engage in activities in a variety of different spheres or contexts and (2) Each of these contexts is governed by a distinct set of norms. Nissenbaum argues that "norms affecting these two principles both shape and limit our roles, behavior, and expectations by governing the flow of personal information in a given context" (2004, p. 137). This is different than traditional views of privacy, which focus on information control (Grodzinsky & Tavani, 2010). Instead, Nissenbaum argues that privacy is not binary, that is, something is private or something is public, but rather depends on the context, the social situation. The two types of informational norms that Nissenbaum mentions are: (a) norms of appropriateness, and (b) norms of distribution. Norms of appropriateness determine whether a certain type of personal information is appropriate or inappropriate to share within a particular context. Norms of distribution restrict the flow of information within and across contexts. According to Nissenbaum, when either of these norms is "breached," a "violation of privacy occurs" (Nissenbaum, 2004, p. 125).

This book draws upon Nissenbaum's research (2010) to further assert that conceptions and expectations of privacy are informed by existing, socially situated conventions, practices and ways of knowing. This book explores the conceptualization of privacy as an evolving social norm. It views privacy exposure as existing on a spectrum, with individuals constantly moving up and down the spectrum as they vary their privacy exposure across different media platforms.

Using Israel as a case study, the book examines the way individuals engage in privacy exposure across four different types of media—reality TV, social networks, blogs and mobile phones—and explores how traditional expectations regarding the value of privacy are being negotiated. Israeli society is wrestling with its collectivist roots, on the one hand, and its individualist ethos, on the other. Israel was founded on the tenets of collectivism and communal nationalism which prioritized, and to some extent continues to prioritize, solidarity and emotional and material sharing over individualism and the private sphere. In recent decades, however, Israeli culture has undergone a period of "Americanization," adopting more liberal, capitalist and individualistic values along with new perceptions of privacy. This process has created a tension, reflected in many aspects of Israeli society, between its collective roots and the desire for individualism. Furthermore, as a country heavily influenced by Western values, yet situated in the Middle East, Israel provides valuable insight into the changes currently occurring in both the Arab and Western worlds, and, as a result of its rapid technological development, serves as a case study for changes that are poised to occur in Western societies in the future.

Israel is characterized as a "startup nation" both for its infatuation with and adoption of new technologies, particularly in the realm of communication. Israel's Internet adoption rates are among the highest around the world, providing a prime opportunity for evaluating changes in privacy perceptions and expectations in other societies. With Israelis quickly adopting the latest new media technologies, whether Facebook or reality TV's "Big Brother," at ever-increasing rates, Israeli society's expectations of privacy, and levels and types of privacy exposure are constantly being negotiated.

Part of Israeli societal views on privacy can be traced back to Jewish religious tradition, which manifests the idea that one is never by himself, but is always being watched by God (Rakover, 2006). Thus, the individual essentially cannot experience "pure" privacy or intimacy, in the sense of being completely alone (Rakover, 2006; Kemelman, 2013). As in the words of the Jewish sages: "Know what is above from you: a seeing eye, a listening ear, and all your deeds being inscribed in a book" (Ethics of the Fathers: Ch. 2). Therefore, not only are one's actions being observed, but also his thoughts and feelings are exposed to the divinity, as expressed in the term often used to describe God, "bochen kelayot valev" ("Who seest the thoughts and the mind" {Book of Jeremiah, 11, 20}).

However, Jewish scripture does devote noticeable attention to the necessity of a personal domain, and the obligation to protect and maintain it, hundreds of years before this idea first appeared in Western legal literature (Aharoni-Goldenberg, 2013). The Hebrew law defines a man's right to physical privacy, prohibiting invasion of one's home (Baba Bathra 17b). The Halacha, the collection of Jewish law, also protects what is recognized in modern literature as informational privacy, and forbids the dissemination of one's private information, or any action to gather such information. (Aharoni-Goldenberg, 2013). This normative obligation relies on several sources, the most notable is "Lo telech rechil be-ameicha" ("You shall not go up and down as a talebearer among your people" {Leviticus, 19, 16}) according to which, one should not spread any personal information about another person, even when true and not offensive.

Thus, the combination of Jewish tradition, collectivist roots and rapid technological adoption makes Israel an insightful and fascinating case study into the evolving nature of our perceptions of privacy in the new media age.

The book is divided into six main chapters. The first two chapters (*Introduction* and *What is Privacy?*) will provide a review of relevant literature and establish the general foundation for the following four chapters. The four chapters are divided according to media type: reality television, social media, online blogs and mobile phones. Each chapter provides a theoretical overview and an empirical analysis based on the privacy exposure typology developed by the authors. Chapter 7 conclusively outlines the discussion as a whole.

The information and communications revolution has changed social perceptions regarding the concept of privacy, creating new models of behavior and imitation. The media both reflect and shape our conceptions of privacy and express the many changes taking place in this area. The media invades the privacy of all of us, yet at the same time they play a critical role in both shaping our understanding of privacy and redrawing the boundaries between the private and public "space."

Symptoms of privacy loss are prevalent across media platforms, including TV, online and mobile all over the world, as well as in Israel. In this book we examine privacy exposure across these mediums and find that more and more individuals are exposing more and more of their personal information in this public space. Moreover, deeper changes are taking place regarding the meaning and value attributed to privacy. Privacy, once considered an important value worthy of respect and protection, has now been replaced with an increased need for personal exposure and a growing desire to penetrate the privacy of others, seemingly without limit nor effort.

Privacy changes in the Israeli context are examined as a model for other phenomena occurring worldwide. Israel is an example of a country which is rapidly adopting communication technologies and, at the same time, quickly losing its privacy. Conclusively, the book displays how Israeli society, through its rapid adoption of new media technologies and increasing levels of privacy exposure, is returning to its collectivist roots and manifesting (or rather its members manifest) a desire to belong to the "community."

These new social perceptions and conceptions of privacy have been reflected, shaped and made possible by technological changes, creating an interesting phenomenon which is not only reflected in the public sphere, but influences all social interactions: personal, familial, intimate and the like. We have created new circles of privacy—friends, family, work—whose boundaries are increasingly blurred, giving way to "privacy leakages." Such leakages are, in and among themselves, an expression of privacy loss. Our traditional desire to maintain a sense of privacy has disappeared and given way to new interpretations of privacy.

This book applies a privacy typology to offer a deeper, more nuanced examination of privacy exposure across media platforms—breaking down privacy exposure according to precise levels and types. This is the first time that privacy exposure has been analyzed and divided according to these criteria. It shows that the accelerated model taking place in Israel is a prophetic model for similar changes occurring in the rest of the world. In a conclusive opinion, while the increasing loss of privacy and the changes in our values and in the meaning of privacy do have detrimental consequences, there are also many positive outcomes. Disclosure, transparency, acceptance of others, and an increasing sense of support and community can sometimes compensate for the loss of control and autonomy that result from the invasion of privacy. The new world is a world without traditional conceptions of privacy. One should acclimatize—forever cognitive of both the benefits as well as the detriments.

REFERENCES

Altman, I. (1975). *The environment and social behavior: Privacy, personal space, territory, crowding.* Monterey, Calif: Brooks/Cole Publishing.

Altman, I. (1977). Privacy regulation: Culturally universal or culturally specific? *Journal of Social Issues, 33*(3), 66–84.

Boyd, D. (2011). Dear voyeur, meet flâneur . . . Sincerely, social media. *Surveillance & Society, 8*(4), 505–507. Retrieved from: http://library.queensu.ca/ojs/index.php/surveillance-and-society/article/viewFile/4187/4189

Buchanan, T., Paine, C., Joinson, A.N., & Reips, U. (2007). Development of measures of online privacy concern and protection for use on the internet. *Journal of the American Society for Information Science and Technology, 58*(2), 157–165.

Cohen, J.E. (2012). *Configuring the networked self: Law, code, and the play of everyday practice.* New Haven: Yale University Press.

Decrew, J.W. (1997). *In pursuit of privacy: law, ethics and the rise of technology.* Ithaca, NY: Cornell University Press.

Grodzinsky, F.S., & Tavani, H. T. (2010). Applying the "contextual integrity" model of privacy to personal blogs in the blogosphere. *International Journal of Internet Research and Ethics, 3*(12) 38–47.

Johnson, B. (2010, January 11). Privacy no longer a social norm, says Facebook founder. *The Guardian.* Retrieved from: http://www.theguardian.com/technology/2010/jan/11/facebook-privacy on January 5, 2014.

Katsh, E. (1989). *The electronic media and the transformation of law.* Oxford: Oxford University Press.

Lehikoinen, J.T. (2008). Theory and application of the privacy regulation model. In J. Lumsden (Ed.). *Handbook of research on user interface design and evaluation for mobile technology.* Canada: National Research Council of Canada.

McGrath, J.E. (2004). *Loving big brother: Performance, privacy and surveillance space.* London: Routledge.

Nissenbaum, H. (2004). Privacy as contextual integrity. *Washington Law Review, 79*(1), 119–157.

Nissenbaum, H. (2010). *Privacy in context: Technology, policy, and the integrity of social life.* Stanford, CA: Stanford University Press.

Orwell, G. (1949). *1984.* London: Secker and Warburg.

Rosen, J. (2000). *The unwanted gaze: The destruction of privacy in America.* New York: Random House, Inc.

Rössler, B. (2005). *The value of privacy.* Cambridge: Polity Press.

Sarvas, R., & Frohlich D.M. (2011). *From snapshot to social media: the changing picture of domestic photography.* Springer, London.

Segal, Z. (1983). The right to privacy vs. the right to know. *Tel Aviv University Law Review* 1, 175.

Smith, C. (2015, May 4). "By the numbers: 200+ amazing Facebook user statistics (April 2015)." *Digital marketing stats.* Retrieved from: http://expandedramblings. com/index.php/by-the-numbers-17-amazing-facebook-stats/ on May 8, 2015.

Steeves, V. (2009). Reclaiming the social value of privacy. In I. Kerr, V. Steeves & C. Lucock (Eds.), *Privacy, identity and anonymity in a network world: Lessons from the identity trail.* New York: Oxford University Press. Retrieved from http:// www.idtrail.org/files/ID%20Trail%20Book/9780195372472_kerr_11.pdf

Tomescu, M., & Trofin, L. (2011). Identity, security and privacy in the information society. *Contemporary Readings in Law & Social Justice, 2*(2), 307–312.

Tufekci, Z. (2008). Can you see me now? Audience and disclosure regulation in online social network sites. *Bulletin of Science, Technology & Society, 28*(1), 20–36.

Chapter 2

The Notion of Privacy

The concept of privacy is ambiguous and vaguely understood. Often used in day-to-day conversations, media reports and political discussions, as well as in legal and philosophical fields, privacy is interpreted and understood across a range of dimensions, and its conceptualizations and definitions differ quite frequently. Is privacy primarily a universal value that should be safeguarded against threats raised by modern technology or is it mainly one's control over his/her public image and personal details and exposure? Is privacy a universal notion that exists similarly in all human beings or is it embedded in a social and cultural context, shaped by local norms and subjective sensibilities?

The following chapter explores the different conceptions of privacy suggested in current literature, so as to understand privacy theory regarding research and to lay the theoretical basis for discussion.

PRIVACY AS A MATTER OF CONTROL OR A CONDITION?

Privacy as a Matter of Control

The concept of privacy has roots in early philosophical discussions. Notably, most Greek philosophers distinguish between the "public" domain of political activity and the private sphere associated with family and domestic life (Moore, 1984). The words for private and public have existed in both Eastern and Western cultures since ancient times (Newell, 1995, p. 88). Modern examinations of the concept of privacy can be traced back to the beginning of the previous century, in George Simmel's account of the nature of the public and the private (Margulis, 1977, p. 5). Simmel considered privacy as having to do with "control of stimulus input from others, degree of mutual knowledge and separateness of people from one another" (Simmel, cited by Altman, 1974, p. 5)

A significant share of the privacy literature may be classified as "control-based," stating that privacy has to do with control over access to oneself. This is in contrast with other scholars who define privacy primarily as a conditional matter, as a state of affairs (Segev, 2010). These two approaches exemplify the wide range of differing views over the term "privacy." Another distinction should be made between approaches that focus on bodily privacy, which is, "to control access to one's body, capacities and powers," and informational privacy, which stresses the importance of control over information about oneself (Moore, 2003, p. 215).

Parker (1973, p. 281) encompasses both bodily and informative privacy, defining it as "control over when and by whom the various parts of us can be sensed by others, where "sensed" is simply seen, touched, smelled or tasted, and "parts of us" refers to the parts of our bodies, our voices, the products of our bodies and objects that are closely associated with us." This definition is consistent with some of our intuitive claims about the things we own. Let's say, for example, that someone has, without permission, used another person's blank paper that contains no information or details. Consistent with Parker's definition of privacy, we may say that by using the paper, some of this person's property rights were violated, but his privacy was not harmed or intruded upon. Using the same approach, Moore (2003, p. 218) defines privacy as a "certain level of control over the inner spheres of personal information and access to one's body, capacities and powers."

Lehikoinen (2008, p. 864) defines privacy as "the measure of control an individual has over information about him/herself or over intimacies of personal identity, or over who has sensory access to him/her." In essence, privacy is an issue of access: To be private is to control or regulate the level of access that the outside world has to one's personal property, body, or thoughts (Kitzmann, 2004).

Westin (1967), in his seminal account of privacy, identified privacy with personal control over personal information, emphasizing the importance of choice in these matters. "Privacy is the claim of individuals, groups or institutions to determine for themselves when, how, and to what extent information about themselves is communicated to others. (. . .). Privacy is the voluntary and temporary withdrawal of a person from general society throughout physical or psychological means" (p. 7). Ittelson et al. also conceptualized privacy in terms of autonomy, arguing that "the root quality of privacy, whether it is achieved by structuring the physical environment or by virtue of how a person relates to others who are continually present, lies in its capacity to maximize the individuals' freedom of choice" (1974, p. 161). Additionally, this notion was analyzed by Mayer-Schönberger (2011); he emphasized that "the Internet insists on remembering what we sometime have chosen to forget" (p. 4). This is part of the discussion revolving around the changing nature of privacy in the digital age. An essential notion that relates to the concept of "privacy as autonomy" is the changing balance between forgetting and remembering.

Jourard (1966) emphasized a person's desire to withhold information about him or herself. "Privacy is an outcome of a person's wish to withhold from others certain knowledge as to his past and present experience and action and his intentions for the future" (p. 307). Foddy and Finighan (1981) argued that "privacy is the possession by an individual of control over information that would interfere with the acceptance of his claims for an identity within a pacified role relationship" (p. 6), while Altman (1975, p. 18) maintained that privacy is "the selective control over access to the self."

As mentioned, one can identify two elements that emerge in the discussion, consistent with Moore's distinction. The first is control over access to information inter alia about how one wishes to shape his/her personality, the way he is perceived, and what information others know about him. Second is the perception of privacy as a physical space that should not be intruded upon. In this view, privacy is the control over inputs from others or from the environment, namely, having a space that should not be disturbed, and that is physically separated and normatively immune to intrusions (bathrooms / medical tests / etc.). Some scholars developed a concept of invisible area, a personal space called the "bubble," which is "the area that if entered by another without invitation—constituted an invasion of privacy" (Newell, 1995, p. 91). Later we will see that these distinctions are consistent with individuals' understanding and expectations of privacy.

Related to the control-based concept, some scholars have defined privacy as a form of autonomy over personal matters and self-realization. Ozer and colleagues (2010) have written that "privacy gives us the autonomy to address sensitive issues without fear of exposure, the ability to explore facets of our personality and individuality, and the power to form close bonds with some by excluding others." Westin (1967) thought of privacy as "an instrument for achieving individual goals for self realization" (as cited in Newell, 1995, p. 88). This approach, which defines privacy as having to do with control over personal space and information, seems to imply that conditions of complete exposure, if entered voluntarily, are in fact another form of privacy, which is by no means consistent within our intuitions and expectations relating to privacy.

Privacy as a Condition

Different from the control-based approach, several scholars have perceived privacy primarily as a state of affairs, in which one's specific and defined personal information is not accessible to others (e.g., sexual practices). It is not necessarily a position of control to the extent to which one is separated from others, but rather the degree of being separated from others, that is, a certain domain of details and information which is protected and separated from others.

Parent (1983) and Segev (2010) have supported this approach, describing the inconsistencies of definitions focusing on control and choice. As Parent successfully demonstrated, a person who voluntarily exposes intimate information about himself is "by all means 'exercising' control," but one "should not say that in doing so she is preserving or protecting her privacy. On the contrary—she is voluntarily relinquishing much of her privacy" (p. 273). Parent therefore defined privacy as "the condition of not having undocumented personal knowledge about one, possessed by others" (p. 269). But this definition is not sensitive to the major concerns of privacy, as Moore has argued, since what is disputed is exactly the thing that should stay undocumented, and because what is publicly available information may be dependent upon technology (pp. 217–218). Moreover, as Segev has written, dissemination of information, even if documented, may indeed intrude upon one's privacy.

Segev (2010) argued against a binary conception, stating that one's privacy can still be invaded even when previously exposed information is once again exposed. In his view, leaked intimate photos of a celebrity with a history of nearly nude campaigns is indeed an invasion of privacy (p. 54). Segev's view of privacy mainly as the absence of personal information about oneself is not shared by others (pp. 51–53). However, for this definition to be useful, it is imperative to define what is considered personal information.

Schoeman (1984) has provided a similar but more comprehensive definition. A person has privacy (rather than exercises it) "to the extent that others have limited access to information about him/her (. . .), to intimacies of his/her life (. . .), to his/her thoughts or body" (p. 3). Rosen (2000) described privacy by the specific content that should characterize private space. "We should preserve private spaces for those activities about which there are legitimately varying views, activities that no one in a civilized society should be forced to submit to public scrutiny" (as cited in Post, 2001, p. 2094).

Among more psychologically based definitions of privacy, we find Velecky who viewed privacy as "a state in which persons may find themselves," where "being alone" is the closest notion to this conception, and Fischer, who stated that "privacy occurs when the watching self and the world fall away (. . .) along with other contingencies" (cited in Newell, 1995, p. 89).

But these definitions appear to be too conclusive and narrow, so as to erase possible differences regarding the information accessible to others, between people who enjoy privacy, and thus disable the ability to generalize a definition that would be methodologically useful. By defining privacy merely as a situation or condition of separation, we miss a crucial element of privacy, which is the state of mind of the individual, and as such, the actual experience of privacy. Some definitions seem to mix both aspects in an attempt to solve this inadequacy. They define privacy in a control-based fashion, which then leads to a condition of separation. Privacy, accordingly, is not merely about control or choice, and not merely about separation, but involves both aspects.

According to Rule (2007), for example, "privacy is the exercise of an authentic option to withhold information on one's self." Privacy by this definition is therefore not merely one's control over personal space, but the actual exercising of the option to "withhold." As Rule argues, "a calculating celebrity may have every means of keeping her life to herself but throw privacy to the winds, living flamboyantly in hopes of drawing the attention of curious fans" (p. 3). The celebrity, accordingly, does not experience privacy. Conversely presented, one can be in a condition of physical separation, with limited access to his/her private space and information, yet that should not be regarded as a situation of privacy if one does not choose to be in that condition, controlling and defining one's privacy. Under this approach, we find Weinstein's definition of privacy as a condition of voluntary seclusion or walling off (Moore, 2003, p. 219).

These definitions are useful in distinguishing between different situations of solitude, seclusion or separation. Unlike conditions entered involuntarily, privacy is a condition of voluntary separation. When entered involuntarily, we may say that one is in a condition of isolation when caused by circumstances, and in a condition of ostracism when caused by the choices of others (Weinstein, 1971, p. 94). According to Kelvin, isolation denotes the negative aspects of separateness, while privacy denotes its positive ones (Newell, 1995, p. 92). Simply put, privacy carries a value. Velecky acknowledged that privacy implies that this state is regarded as valuable, while just "being alone" carries no such implication (Newell, 1995, p. 89). Westin (1967) proposed similarly to view privacy as divided into different sorts, reflecting attitudes on the part of the individual. For example, anonymity is defined as "a type of privacy that occurred when it was possible to move around in public without being recognized or the subject of attention."

The Legal Discussion and the Right to Privacy

Brandeis and Warren (1890) laid the basis for a primary notion of privacy that was subsequently endorsed by the courts and the state and developed into shaping the right to privacy. The meanings of privacy derived from the legal literature therefore reflect similar conceptions and approaches.

Legal scholar Prosser (1960) identified four distinct torts that reflect different types of privacy claims in order to draw up a general concept of privacy derived from the law and expressing general acceptance: intrusion upon a person's seclusion, solitude or personal affairs in a highly offensive manner; personal disclosure, namely, publicizing highly offensive private information about someone which is not of legitimate concern to the public; "false light"—casting someone publicly in a false light; and the appropriation of another's name or likeness for some advantage without the other's consent (as cited by Moore, 2003, p. 215). O'reilly (1984) mentioned that "the constitutionally protected concept of privacy is a sphere of space that a man may carry around with him, which is protected from outside intrusion, as a right of selected disclosure about oneself, and as a right of personal autonomy" (Newell, 1995, p. 91).

Yael Onn and colleagues (2005, p. 26) have argued that the right to privacy is "the right to maintain our personal space," which includes all things that are part of us, such as thoughts, feelings, secrets, identity, body and home. According to them, the right to privacy is the ability to both decide which parts of this personal space can be accessed by others and to "control the extent, manner and timing for using those parts we decided to expose" (Onn et al., 2005, p. 26). Birnhack and Elkin-Koren (2009, p. 5) have presented and explained two main approaches—European and American, for deciding which privacy policies should be adopted. They write that the European approach heavily regulates any collection and processing of personal information, whereas the American approach tends to advocate a more "hands off" position, except for particular kinds of data, such as credit information, health information, or data collected from children under the age of thirteen (Birnhack & Elkin-Koren, 2009, p. 5).

Israeli law has adopted a wide definition of the term privacy, defining it as an individual's interest in not being bothered in his private life by others (Segal, 1983). Yet it has acknowledged that the right's scope is dim and changes in accordance with changes in reality (Supreme Court decision 1211/96).

Inadequacies of defining privacy often arise when the right to privacy is confused with the notion of privacy itself. Parent (1983) implies that by stressing the element of control, scholars strive to actually define the right to privacy and on what condition it is violated, rather than the condition of privacy itself. Segev (2010, p. 38) stressed the importance of the distinction between the two. To clarify this point, we may use the following example: When an intimate discussion between a couple is being overheard by someone who has employed a device in their home—their privacy is invaded through the violation of their right to privacy. However, if their personal information is exposed to a random person walking by their home and hearing their loud conversation through an open window, we may say that their privacy has indeed been harmed, or that they enjoy less privacy, in the sense that some of the intimate details existing in their private space have been exposed, but no right has been violated.

IS THERE A COHERENT NOTION OF PRIVACY?

By referring to some of the main accounts set to shape a coherent notion of the right to privacy, we may learn a lot about privacy itself, as perceived by legal scholars, and specifically, about two main approaches to the core notion of the term that stands at the basis of a great extent of the literature. It goes as follows: If the definitions and meanings of privacy vary significantly, is it possible to derive an overarching concept of privacy? Or is it rather just several distinct notions that have been lumped together?

Some have argued that the definitional variability could be a reflection of different dimensions and expectations or interpretations of one common notion. The position that there is something common to most of the claims was referred to by Schoeman as the "coherence thesis" (Schoeman, 1984, p. 5). By contrast, some have argued that what we refer to as privacy is reducible to claims of other kinds. To elaborate on this option, we should explore some of the literature regarding the right to privacy.

Thomson's conception of the right to privacy (1975) is perhaps the most well-known critical account of the concept. Thomson described privacy as a bundle of rights, all overlapping with rights of another—those of a more fundamental kind, such as property rights, to name one. According to Thomson, "I don't have a right to not be looked at because I have a right to privacy— one is inclined rather to say that it is because I have these (other) rights, that I have a right to privacy." In other words, privacy is regarded as a derivative consequence of maintaining other fundamental rights. "It is possible to explain each right in the cluster, without ever once mentioning the right to privacy" (Thomson, 1975, pp. 312–313). Davis similarly stated that "invasion of privacy is, in reality, a complex of more fundamental wrongs. Similarly the individual's interest in privacy itself is derivative" (Davis quoted in Moore, 1984, p. 217). Is Moore correct in maintaining that privacy rights are simply a special form of property rights?

Scanlon (1975), in response to Thomson's paper, argued that the diverse cases of what we perceive as violations of privacy rights do share a common foundation, which is "the special interests that we have in being able to be free from certain kinds of intrusions" (Scanlon, 1975, p. 5). Scanlon provides an interesting hypothetical case: "An x-ray device is used to examine an object in one's safe. The right that is violated, so he argues, does not depend on owning the object, but on the zone of privacy invaded. It could be another person's object, but that doesn't remove the wrongfulness of the intrusion" (p. 319).

Privacy, according to Scanlon, is therefore "a zone, that should be protected by our conventions and laws, in which we can carry out our activities without the necessity of being continually alert for possible observers, listeners, etc." (p. 316). That is to say, our conventions and laws of what are considered privacy violations are in fact defining this "territory" of privacy, immune from specified interventions.

Margulis (1977) suggested a definition, which, according to him, is sufficient to serve as an "abstract skeleton" for varying meanings and expectations regarding what should be considered as private. "Privacy, as a whole or in part, represents the control of transactions between person(s) and other(s), the ultimate aim of which is to enhance autonomy and/or to minimize vulnerability" (Margulis, 1977, p. 10). Moore (1984, p. 217) argued "that the cluster of rights that comprise privacy may find their roots in property or liberty, yet still mark out a distinct kind." Gavison (1980) suggested that privacy be viewed as a complex concept comprised of three independent and irreducible elements: solitude, anonymity and secrecy.

Segev (2010, p. 32) mentioned that a considerable extent of the literature on privacy contains a normative component in addition to the conceptual one; for example, defining privacy by its necessity to preserve human dignity; the perception of privacy as a "supremely important human good, as a value somehow at the core of what makes life worth living;" or the view that "privacy is fundamental to our personhood." Ozer and colleagues (2010) asserted that, as individuals, "privacy gives us the autonomy to address sensitive issues without fear of exposure, the ability to explore facets of our personality and individuality, and the power to form close bonds with some by excluding others." Privacy makes it possible for a healthy society to experiment and grow while safeguarding the balance between individual liberties and government powers—and is considered by many as a fundamental building block of a robust democracy.

Privacy for Itself—or an Instrument for Other Goals

A somehow related discussion concerns the kind of interests that move people to withhold information about themselves. Rule (2007, p. 4) made a distinction between purely "instrumental motives," where, for example, people choose to withhold information about themselves to achieve practical advantages or disadvantages; and intrinsic motives, where people gain "inherent satisfaction at keeping certain information and experiences to one's self." He contended that "if privacy is often a means to strategic ends, it can also be an end in itself (. . .). There are moments in life that people choose not to share even though everyone knows that they occur (. . .). Most people would probably prefer not to share with others records of embarrassing medical procedures they have undergone—even when everyone understands that the procedures have taken place."

Rule (2007, p. 6) also referred to a holistic value of privacy. "We often stand to gain or lose from widely experienced gains or losses to privacy, regardless of what happens to information about ourselves individually. If nearly everyone around me feels and acts as though all conversations were overheard, then something crucial is lost from public life—even if I am convinced that my own conversations are secure."

Is Privacy Culturally Relative?

Having a broader understanding of the concept of privacy, one should still discuss its varying manifestations across and within cultures. To be more specific, we should understand to what extent privacy is culturally relative. Even if we agree on a shared conception of an element of privacy, let's say, control over access to one's private domain—different people exercise it differently. They enjoy privacy in varied settings and manners, have different expectations and claims, and gain a sense of privacy in different situations. Individuals, especially across cultures, differ in what they choose to withhold and how they regulate their interactions with others. *Societies differ in what is in fact thought to be private, and what should be protected from public scrutiny.* Schoeman (1984, p. 6) has asked two salient questions regarding cultural variation. Is privacy important to all people? Are any aspects of life inherently private and not just conventionally so? We shall therefore investigate how people and cultures differ in their sensitivity to privacy issues, and to what extent the criteria of the private varies across societies.

Moore (1984, p. 215) stated that there is a "near universal need for privacy." Rule (2007, p. 3) argued that privacy concerns are universal, that "it is impossible to imagine a social world where people are indifferent to the potential consequences of sharing information about themselves that only they know (. . .) In every social setting, people stand to gain or lose by controlling what others know about them, and certainly by keeping certain personal information to themselves." Westin (1967) noted the biological basis of privacy when he argued that "a man's need for privacy may well be rooted in his animal origins."

Newell (1998) explored the commonalities among respondents from different cultures to privacy perceptions and usage. The results show that the majority of all three cultures examined, (students from Ireland, Senegal and the United States), considered privacy to be a condition of the person, that is, they perceived privacy as primarily a "cognitive or affective state of the individual." Moreover, most of the participants claimed to seek privacy under similar conditions and agreed that the most important facet of privacy was "not being disturbed."

However, privacy does take different forms. Whitman (2004, pp. 1153–1154) wrote that "the sense of what must be kept private, of what must be hidden before the eyes of others, seems to differ strangely from society to society, and shifted and mutated over time." Privacy expectations in a small town thus differ from those in a metropolis. Rule (2007, p. 3) argued that "every social world entails its distinctive patterns on withholding and disclosure. The personal data one expects to share with government agencies in an expansive welfare state like Sweden differs vastly from what one expects in the United States."

Studies indeed affirm the importance of cultural context in the structuring of privacy expectations and interests. Studies show that the private sphere of an individual in India might include the whole familial space. It would therefore be plausible for a practitioner to discuss patient information of the wife with her husband or family, a practice that would be regarded as violation of the patient's privacy in some European countries (Parekh, 2009).

Newell (1995, p. 97) mentioned that "cultural differences in attitudes towards privacy were documented in the anthropological literature." The differences identified existed in "styles of privacy" or "mechanisms for obtaining privacy," but nearly every culture sought some type of privacy (Newell, 1995, p. 88).

According to Newell, several cultures do not even possess a term equivalent to privacy in their language. Such an absence has been identified in Arabic, Dutch, Japanese, Russian, and some tribal societies. She states that "privacy is culturally relative, depending on social and political values of a certain society or domain (. . .). The desire for privacy takes different forms and magnitude from culture to culture according to a range of factors."

Birnhak (2010, p. 38) stated that a society's history, culture and practices greatly influence the right to privacy endorsed by its legal system, and the things that are considered to be private. For example, Whitman (2004, p. 1155) argued that "some of the things that bother French and German observers, involve what Americans will think of as trivialities of everyday behavior." Conversely, many European practices seem intuitively objectionable to Americans. "If the Europeans are puzzled by the ill-bred way which Americans casually talk about themselves, Americans are puzzled by the ill-bred way in which Europeans casually take off their clothes" (Whitman, 2004, p. 1158).

According to Whitman, the fundamental contrast is between two conceptions of privacy—as an aspect of dignity and as an aspect of liberty. The European privacy protections are, at their core, rights to one's image, name and reputation. By contrast, America is much more oriented toward values of liberty, specifically—liberty against the state. The primary danger from an American point of view is that "the sanctity of our home will be breached by government actors" (Whitman, 2004, p. 1162). This is why American anxieties often focus on maintaining a kind of private sovereignty within one's own walls.

It is important to note that within cultures, privacy expectations indeed differ between people, and may change over time. Several scholars suggested that some people may have a greater need for privacy than others. Birnhak (2010, p. 46) demonstrated how privacy expectations in the big city and the small village differ. In some sense, one enjoys more privacy in the village, having more natural spaces and less crowded surroundings. On the other hand, in the city, there is greater alienation, enabling one to enjoy more anonymity and to be less exposed.

Wolfe and Laufer (1974) explored the "different meanings, functions and behavioral referents" of the concept of privacy across diverse user groups. Thirty-nine different uses were distinguished among children and adolescents, including controlling access to information, being alone, no one bothering me, controlling access to spaces, and others. According to Newell (1995, p. 87), it was also suggested by several different authors that "definitions of privacy changed as a function of the development of the individual and the specific environmental context." While everyone has deplored the invasion of privacy *in principle* (Tomescu and Trofin, 2010, p. 308), Steeves (2008) argued that privacy is a dynamic, individualistic, and socially constructed process that changes over time.

Privacy as Boundary-Control

This book builds in part upon social psychologist Irwin Altman's (1975) theory of privacy as a set of "interpersonal boundary-control processes" by which an individual decides, and asserts control over how much personal information to reveal to others. This process is dialectical because contact and exposure are both restricted and sought, and ultimately optimized in order to achieve a desired balance. In other words, Altman observed that individuals engage in a range of privacy-regulating behaviors, and that together, these behaviors constitute a coherent system for personal boundary management that responds dynamically to changing circumstances needs, and desires. According to Altman, privacy is "a central regulatory process by which a person (or group) makes himself more or less accessible and open to others" (Cohen, 2012, p. 131). Therefore, for Altman (1975), more privacy is not necessarily the goal. Rather, he asserts that there is an "optimal degree of desired access of the self to the others at any moment in time" (p. 11). Altman's work showed that privacy-regulating behaviors mediate human interaction both physically and conceptually.

Adopting Altman's view of privacy as a "selective control of access to the self," it is necessary to explore the boundary negotiations, especially the "disclosure nondisclosure boundary," by examining how individuals engage in privacy exposure across four different types of media platforms, specifically, reality TV, online social networks (OSN), blogs, and mobile phones.

PRIVACY LOSS

Reality TV, social networks, mobile phones, and blogs are all founded on the willingness of individuals to share their personal information, their photos, political affinities and locations, thoughts and feelings with the general public. Moreover, the standardization of information available by digital storage devices has made it possible to share, distribute and store this information, irrespective of the type of content, in the same digital network (Mayer-Schönberger, 2011). According to Mayer-Schönberger and Kenneth Cukier, "big data analytics are revolutionizing the way we see and process the world" (Kakutani, 2013, par. 8).

This "big data revolution" means that mass amounts of information that individuals share may be stored for an unlimited period of time by companies such as Google, Facebook, Twitter, and the like. This raises potential implications related to privacy loss, as in Mayer-Schönberger words—"if we had to worry that any information about us would be remembered for longer than we live—would we still express our views on matters of trivial gossip, share personal experiences, make various political comments, or would we self censor?" (Mayer-Schönberger, 2011, p. 5).

According to Mayer-Schönberger (2011), few people who use digital technology understand that every move, preference, behavior, and, namely, every piece of data about them—is being recorded, preserved for years and available to third parties (pp. 1–16). For example, Google, which holds a massive amount of search terms, is able to connect search queries to a particular individual across time, by combining login data cookies and IP addresses. "Google knows more about us than we can remember ourselves" (Mayer-Schönberger, 2011, p. 7). So what should consumers do about this? Mayer-Schönberger argues that individuals should learn to forget, as well as to customize privacy settings with an expiration date for certain documents and information (a specific time for when that information will be deleted).

An individual's privacy and autonomy are perceived to have critical weight in one's ability to keep his identity and consolidate loving, close and trusting relationships with those surrounding him, as well as consolidating a public and political identity (Gavison, 1988). Thus, the loss of privacy is generally perceived as a disaster, as characteristic of an inhuman and totalitarian

Check-Out Receipt

Alameda Free Library
Main Branch
1550 Oak Street
Alameda, CA
www.alamedafree.org
Tel: 510-747-7777

Checkout Date: 11-4 -2016 - 14:35:29

Patron ID.: xxxxxxxxxx6970

---

1 Terms of service : social media
33341007840563   Due Date: 11/26/16

Total Items: 1

Balance Due: $ 0.00

Check us out on social media!
Twitter: @alamedafree
Facebook: facebook.com/alamedafreelibrary

society. The most prominent example is, of course, described in George Orwell's novel, *1984* (Orwell, 1949). The book portrays a dystopian world whose inhabitants have virtually no real privacy. Many of the citizens live under constant surveillance, residing in apartments equipped with two-way tele screens so that they may be watched or listened to at any time.

However, this scenario is no longer so far-fetched. In fact, it seems to reflect many changes that have taken place in developed countries in which the individual is accustomed to living under supervision (McGrath, 2004). Cameras watch over us en route to our daytime activities; film our license plates and record our movements within stores. Data from banks, from our credit cards and from Internet websites are analyzed in order to gain insight into our shopping habits and our credit history. Internal government agents analyze our phone calls looking for key words that may indicate subversion. "You are under surveillance" is no longer a statement directed at chosen individuals, but a description of our culture. The broad uses of surveillance can justify invasion of privacy, the claim being that surveillance is necessary as a tool enabling crime prevention. However, in some cases, surveillance tools simply enable governments or commercial bodies to access information about us, strengthening their power and control over our lives. Thus, the "right to privacy," just as the concept itself, is relative and depends upon culture, society, time and place.

The court defines the right to privacy according to what is socially acceptable, or in better terms, in accordance with an individual's probable expectations regarding his privacy (Spencer, 2002). Such expectations are constantly changing and are subject to negotiation in a "privacy market" as well as being open to manipulation by other powerful and influential factors. The claim for privacy competes against values and other heavyweight social interests, such as the public's "right to know" and "freedom of speech," which also include freedom of information and freedom of the press, and even the right to watch others (Calvert, 2004). It must be noted that there are also opponents who argue that advocating for the right to privacy is ineffective and only raises the price of information that may be essential for worthy personal and social decisions (Posner, 1978). They claim that too broad a defense of privacy also means harming freedom of speech and freedom of information flow, and enables the powerful and those in authority to hide significant events and information from the public.

Surveys report that ordinary people experience a relatively high general concern about privacy loss, but a low level of concern about the data generated by individual transactions, movements, and communications (Cohen, 2012). Indeed, for most citizens engaged in day-to-day transactions, "convenience often outweighs the theoretical possibility that personal information may be disclosed to strangers" (Rosen, 2000, p. 197). Moreover, we regularly see individuals, whether on TV or online, exposing varying degrees of personal information to a multitude of strangers with seemingly little concern for their personal privacy. Indeed, such personal exposure is desired by many and eagerly pursued. As such, this book argues that traditional privacy is undergoing two processes: On the one hand, traditional notions of privacy are disappearing, while on the other, the concept of privacy itself is being redefined and re conceptualized.

TYPES OF PRIVACY EXPOSURE

Up until now the term "privacy" has been used to convey a number of different types and levels of personal exposure. This book sets out to inform that privacy exposure is multi faceted, that there is a spectrum of ways in which individuals engage and in such ways manage varying degrees of privacy exposure.

As such, a unique typology has developed to address four possible types of exposure that constitute a waiver or loss of privacy. This typology was first developed by Lavie-Dinur and Karniel (2010) and serves as a general framework for analyzing the different ways by which individuals initiate exposure of information.

Privacy Typology

- Factual (Personal) Exposure: Providing personal information and data, such as marital status, financial status, health condition, educational background and employment history, as well as biometric information and data, fingerprints, retinal scans, facial structure recognition and genetic information.
- Visual Exposure: Physical representation by means of photographs, revealing pictures of the body, video clips, and so forth.
- Exposure of Identity and Emotions: Information about private opinions, viewpoints, feelings, principles, religious beliefs and personal characteristics.
- Exposure of Preferences: Individual consumer habits and preferences (with regard to merchandise and food—among others).

It then further explores how privacy exposure is negotiated according to levels of familiarity existing between individuals:

- Level 1, Basic Familiarity: This level of exposure refers to basic information revealed during an initial introduction between two people, such as details about the place of residence, nationality, hobbies and so forth.

- Level 2, Medium Familiarity: This level refers to information revealed between two personal acquaintances consistently over time, although not between close friends. This includes references to the person's family, mood exposure and others.
- Level 3, High Familiarity: This level refers to the type of information revealed between close friends and family. It is defined by relatively high exposure of emotional and personal information, that is, intimate details, etc. It refers to behavior patterns that exist in the private sphere, and requires familiarity between people.
- Level 4, Intimate Familiarity: This level refers to the type of exposure that often occurs between spouses. This exposure level refers to behavior of a sexual nature, and relates to levels of emotional exposure and behavioral patterns generally relegated to the private sphere.

Privacy is a form of opacity, and opacity has its values (Rosen, 2000, p. 224). Privacy norms and practices are complex and dynamic, expressing distinct social and cultural patterns. This book focuses on the changes in the conception and presentation of privacy, accelerated by the emergence of new media technologies, illuminating the shifts, modifications and displacements of the virtual borderline between the private and public space.

Israel is a leader in various sectors of digital use such as rates of online users, patterns of online consumption as well as engagement in social networking. According to research conducted by comSCORE in 2011, 94% of the online population in Israel engage in social networking, compared to 97% in Brazil and 98% in the US, and only 53% in China. More importantly, Israel is ranked first in the total time spent on social network sites with an average of 11.1 hours per visitor (ages 15+) per month. Interestingly, other quick adopters of digital technology, such as Japan and South Korea, showed much lower social network activity and averaged two hours spent on social networking sites per visitor per month.

To illustrate how attitudes and traditional privacy practices compare between Israelis and Americans, Ribak and Turow (2003) have studied and tested attitudes toward web privacy in a cultural context. In the US, the media widely covers matters of privacy and its inherent conflict with technological developments, in sharp contrast to the rare coverage of privacy issues in Israel. According to Ribak and Turow, Israelis show relative tolerance toward privacy violations and information disclosure, and this is consistent with the collectivist foundation of the country's ethos, by which individuals were perceived as members in the project of nation building. Therefore, the line between the personal and collective needs and objectives, and as a result, the boundaries between public and private life are difficult to define. Though the country has indeed undergone processes of privatization and individualization, recurrent national threats continue to strengthen the commitment of Israelis to the collective ethos.

Israel encompasses two significant attributes that fit this book's areas of study. The first is the rapid and vast adoption of digital technology, specifically social networking, that has great importance when investigating the implications of hyper-technology on privacy perceptions within a society. Secondly, Israel's traditional collectivist ethos is characterized by strong cultural norms and by a history of sharing and familiarity. This has led to weaker boundaries between the private and public spheres compared to other individualistic, capitalist and digital technology top-adopter countries. This allows for the opportunity to closely observe an ongoing processes of privacy conceptualization due to technological advances. Since Israeli society draws relatively flexible boundaries in regard to privacy, the changes in privacy perceptions and expectations therefore do not necessarily stand as invasions of the private sphere. This results in individuals who willingly engage in self-exposure and mass-sharing activities (as further elaborated in chapter 6) by utilizing new digital platforms in order to enhance existing social practices and norms, or in other words, redefining privacy according to digital opportunities.

The Israeli case study thus demonstrates how individuals actually behave across various new media, how they perceive the privacy issues inherent in these technologies, and how they actually behave and engage in privacy-exposure thereby ascertaining what privacy ultimately is!

REFERENCES

Altman, I. (1975). *The environment and social behavior: Privacy, personal space, territory, and crowding.* Monterey, Calif: Brooks/Cole Pub. Co.

Birnhack, M., & Elkin-Koren, N. (2009). Does law matter online? Empirical evidence on Privacy law compliance. Social Science Research Network, 5–46.

Birnhack, M. (2010). *Private space: Privacy, law & technology.* Tel Aviv, Israel: Bar Ilan and Nevo Press. [in Hebrew].

Brandeis, L.D., & Warren, S.D. (1890). The right to privacy. *Harvard Law Review, 4*(5), 193–220.

Calvert, C. (2004). Revisiting the voyeurism value in the first amendment: From the sexually sordid to the details of death. *The Seattle University Law Review, 27,* 721.

Cohen, J.E. (2012). *Configuring the networked self: Law, code, and the play of everyday practice.* New Haven: Yale University Press.

Derlega, V.J., & Chaikin, A.L. (1977). Privacy and self-disclosure in social relationships. *Journal of Social Issues, 33*(3), 102–115.

Foddy, W.H. (1981). Obscenity reactions: Toward a symbolic interactionist explanation. *Journal for the Theory of Social Behaviour, 11*(2), 125–146.

Gavison, R. (1980). Privacy and the limits of law. *Yale Law Journal*, 421–471.

Gavison, R. (1988). The rights to privacy and dignity. In A. Swersky (Ed.). *Human rights in Israel: Articles in memory of judge Haman Shelah*. Tel Aviv: Edanim and Yediot Aharonot. (in Hebrew).

Jourard, S.M. (1966). Some psychological aspects of privacy. *Law and Contemporary Problems, 31*, 307.

Kakutani, M. (2013, June 10). Watched by the Web: Surveillance is reborn 'Big Data,' by Viktor Mayer-Schönberger and Kenneth Cukier. *New York Times*. Retrieved on June 7, 2015 from http://www.nytimes.com/2013/06/11/books/big-data-by-viktor-mayer-schonberger-and-kenneth-cukier.html.

Kitzmann, A. (2004). *Saved from oblivion: Documenting the daily from diaries to webcams*. New York: Peter Lang Publishing.

Lehikoinen, J.T. (2008). Theory and application of the privacy regulation model. In J. Lumsden (Ed.). *Handbook of research on user interface design and evaluation for mobile technology*. Canada: National Research Council of Canada.

Margulis, S.T. (1977). Conceptions of privacy: Current status and next steps. *Journal of Social Issues, 33*(3), 5–21.

Mayer-Schönberger, V. (2011). *Delete: The virtue of forgetting in the digital age*. Woodstock, Oxfordshire, UK: Princeton University Press.

Moore, B. (1984). *Privacy: Studies in social and cultural history* (p. 73). New York: ME Sharpe.

Moore, A.D. (2003). Privacy: Its meaning and value. *American Philosophical Quarterly, 40*(3), 215–227.

Newell, P. B. (1995). Perspectives on privacy. *Journal of Environmental Psychology, 15*(2), 87–104.

Newell, P.B. (1998). A cross-cultural comparison of privacy definitions and functions: A systems approach. *Journal of Environmental Psychology, 18*(4), 357–371.

Onn, Y. et al. (2005). *Privacy in the digital environment*. Haifa, Israel: The Haifa Center of Law and Technology Publication Series.

Orwell, G. (1949). *1984*. London: Secker and Warburg.

Ozer, N.A., Conley, C., O'Connell, H., Ginsburg, E., & Gubins, T. (2010). *Location-based services: Time for a privacy check-in*. American Civil Liberties Union (ACLU), San Francisco, CA.

Parekh, B. (2009). Private and public spheres in India. *Critical Review of International Social and Political Philosophy, 12*(2), 313–328.

Parent, W.A. (1983). Privacy, morality, and the law. *Philosophy & Public Affairs*, 269–288.

Parker, R.B. (1973). Definition of privacy. *Rutgers Law Review, 27*, 275.

Post, R.C. (2000). Three concepts of privacy. *Georgetown Law Journal, 89*, 2087.

Posner, R.A. (1978). The right of privacy. *The University of Georgia Law Review, 12*, p. 393.

Rosen, J. (2000). *The unwanted gaze: The destruction of privacy in America*. New York: Random House, Inc.

Rule, J.B. (2007). *Privacy in peril: How we are sacrificing a fundamental right in exchange for security and convenience*. Oxford: Oxford University Press.

Scanlon, T. (1975). Thomson on privacy. *Philosophy & Public Affairs*, 315–322.

Schoeman, F.D. (Ed.). (1984). *Philosophical dimensions of privacy: An anthology.* New York: Cambridge University Press.

Segev, R. (2012). Privacy—Meaning and importance. In T. Altshuler (Ed.), *Privacy in an era of change.* Israel Democracy Institute.

Simmel, G. (1950). *The sociology of Geors Simmel.* (Trans. by K. H. Wolff). New York: The Free Press of Glencoe.

Spencer, S.B. (2002). Reasonable expectations and the erosion of privacy. *The San Diego Law Review, 39,* p. 843.

Thomson, J.J. (1975). The right to privacy. *Philosophy & Public Affairs,* 295–314.

Top 10 need to knows about social networking and where it is headed. (2011, December 21). Retrieved May 13, 2015, from https://www.google.co.il/search?clie nt=safari&rls=en&q=Top 10 Need-to-Knows About Social Networking and Where It's Headed&ie=UTF-8&oe=UTF-8&gfe_rd=cr&ei=hBlTVe2IEciG8Qf1pYHYDg

Whitman, J.Q. (2004). The two western cultures of privacy: Dignity versus liberty. *Yale Law Journal, 113*(6), 1151–1221.

Weinstein, M.A. (1971). The uses of privacy in the good life. *Privacy (Nomos, vol. 13),* 94.

Westin, A.F. (1968). Privacy and freedom. *Washington and Lee Law Review, 25*(1), 166.

Wolfe, M., & Laufer, R. (1974). The concept of privacy in childhood and adolescence. *Privacy,* 29–54.

Chapter 3

Reality TV

Willingly Giving Up Our Privacy for Popularity on the "Big Screen"

Reality television, especially Big Brother, has become a part of the Israeli DNA—everyone knows about it and everyone talks about it. The genre's popularity has grown immensely, comprising 50% of Israeli television programs and leaving the drama genre and the news programs behind with only a minor percentage of airtime (Toker, 2013). Indeed, reality shows like the "Bachelor," "Survival," "Big Brother" and others are Israelis' new addiction. These shows are not scripted, have no stars, and many times simply show ordinary people living their ordinary lives in front of the screen in exchange for a potential prize (Andrejevic, 2004). This growing popularity of reality shows thus leads to questions about how individuals are exposing themselves in this "reality culture." In order to better understand the ways people expose themselves across digital media, the book's typology has been applied to Israeli's Big Brother. The typology examines individuals' factual (personal) exposure, which provides personal information and data; visual exposure that emphasizes physical representation; exposure of identity and emotions: and exposure of individual consumer habits and preferences. The typology will further be analyzed by levels of familiarity ranging from basic familiarity to intimate reality.

Television, while not an online digital technology, has significantly changed the character of society by facilitating the exposure of intimate life events in front of the camera. This is especially true for reality television, which, as Andrejevic (2004) explains, is "the work of being watched." Prior to the inauguration of reality television in 2000, it was hard to imagine people sharing love triangles, family conflicts, addiction problems and other private fields to the scrutinizing eyes of the public. However, since the reality genre has gained popularity, so has the will to expose private matters on television (Marcus, 2015). People began to recognize television as a great platform to manifest their agendas, ideas and ideologies. The new "ideal" was very clear to them—giving away their private affairs for a chance to have social, political and/or economic gain, indeed, without a clear understanding of what this exposure potentially holds in terms of privacy (Lavie-Dinur & Karniel, 2008).

Furthermore, in this book, new norms of behavior and questions regarding the way individuals willingly publish their most private affairs on social networks and/or applications as well as in other forms of digital means, such as television, have been identified. Therefore, the roots of this phenomenon, cannot be ignored.

This book deals with the way people are willing to give up privacy across digital platforms. Nevertheless, in order to comprehend this notion, we must trace the beginning of the process, examining both when and where it began. Reality television became popular before the rise of social networks and digital applications providing an initial indication of change in the view of privacy. Suddenly the private sphere was no longer regarded as sacred, but rather replaced with a desire to be seen and recognized on TV (Mendick, Allen, & Harvey, 2015).

Nowadays it seems common to see having every waking hour of their lives filmed and documented. At the same time, viewers enjoy receiving news and information about reality stars' lives, ranging from celebrations to family dramas and conflicts. This has become a normalized routine of our everyday lives (Johansson, 2015).

Today, the combination of high technology, social network applications, reality culture and other exposure platforms have reshaped the concept of privacy and blurred the border between the public and the private spheres.

ISRAELI REALITY TV: THE BEGINNING OF CHANGE

On December 28, 2010, a noteworthy headline on the popular Israeli Internet gossip site "City Mouse" stated: "Big Brother crosses the limit of privacy!". This statement is a meaningful expression of the changing notion of privacy. The headline referred to the airing of Big Brother Israel the night before.

During the third season, the show's most controversial incident (at the time) occurred when two participants engaged in what seemed to be sexual intercourse on camera. This was the first time in Israeli reality TV history that such an act was broadcast on live television. The act evoked mixed responses from the Israeli public as many journalists, critics and fans alike decried the sexual act, calling it "shameless" and "indecent," while others claimed it was only to be expected.

However, the outcry over the sexual act did not last long. The act, initially described as the most blatant exposure of privacy on Israeli reality television—the physical culmination of participants Lihi Griner and Atay Schulberg's romantic relationship—was soon relegated to the back pages of tabloids, with the public seemingly shrugging the incident off as yet another antic of the reality television genre. After a few weeks, it seemed that the act itself had been "normalized" in the minds of audiences, and would serve, from now on, as the new standard of behavior that reality TV viewers would expect from future participants on the show, and other reality TV shows.

Indeed, like all of the formats of the popular reality show, Big Brother Israel depends on the unfettered exposure of its participants' personal lives. The show's previous seasons (seasons one and two) were fraught with racial and ethnic tensions, featuring participants revealing their personal views about these issues as well as intimate details of their own personal lives. On an important note, racism and racial discrimination seems a common denominator among many countries' reality TV broadcasts (Choi, 2015; Friedman, 2015), and not only in Israel's broadcast of Big Brother. One of the participants in the first season of Big Brother Israel, Yossi Boublil, a contractor of Middle Eastern/North African descent, openly expressed his crude and homophobic views. Boublil even revealed that he had once tried to aggressively lure a girlfriend into group sex—a fact that he had no problem declaring on live television. Furthermore, his daughter, Einav Boublin referred mockingly to the show's Ashkenazi (Eastern European) participants collectively as "the Friedmans" (Kraft, 2008). Past participants have revealed everything from their sexual orientations to feelings and emotions about past relationships, other housemates, politics, and more.

These are just a few of the ways Big Brother Israel participants have chosen to reveal aspects of their private lives to television viewers (Tal-Or & Hershman-Shitrit, 2014). Big Brother participants, and in fact, all reality television participants, are constantly engaging in different types of privacy exposure. What, then, do these different incidents of exposure tell us about the value of privacy? How do we classify the *types* of exposure that participants engage in? The fact that this is the first time in Israeli reality television history that participants engaged in sexual intercourse on the show, broadcasted live, may point to some reservations regarding certain types of privacy exposure among participants. The public's response to the incident may also imply that privacy has a value and that, in this case, Griner and Schulberg went too far in exposing their intimacy to the public.

But more than that, what does this incident tell us about the types of privacy exposure that reality television participants are willing to engage in? That is a question this chapter seeks to explore by delving into the underlying nature and types of such exposure. Such an examination will help in understanding the concept of privacy as it is perceived today.

REALITY TV AS A PRIVACY SPECTRUM

We conducted a study on the Israeli Big Brother program in order to determine whether a correlation existed between greater privacy exposure and success on the show. The study followed the first season of Israel's Big Brother program, which premiered on September 1, 2008. We found that even though participants volunteered to have their lives placed under 24-hour surveillance, they were still cautious about sharing certain aspects of their personal lives. Indeed, participants exercised greater control over their personal details (those that Big Brother cannot "see") in order to avoid exposing themselves completely.

Such findings led to a deeper understanding of privacy as a concept that, far from being absolute, is multi layered and complex. It was noticeable that while some reality TV participants engaged in certain types of exposure, they strictly avoided others, while others did the exact opposite. In order to analyze this, a unique typology to distinctly define and classify these types of privacy exposure was developed.

By asking the questions "what are the characteristics of this exposure on reality television and how is such exposure negotiated among participants?" we are able to focus this chapter on the types of privacy exposure participants engage in.

Over the past two decades, reality TV has become a television phenomenon, transforming programming schedules and occupying a prominent place in the cultural imagery. Meanwhile, research on the subject has struggled to keep pace with the various theoretical and structural challenges that reality TV poses, especially with regard to defining and understanding how viewers and participants perceive what is private and what is public (Murray & Oullette, 2004). Indeed, as van Zoonen (2004) argued, the first season of the Dutch Big Brother reality program had to do with defining the division between two fields—"public life" and "private domain"—as self-evident and worth nurturing. Yet both individuals and reality TV itself have transcended this dichotomy. Individuals willingly broadcast their personal lives on public television and in the same sense, reality television turns private lives of such ordinary people into a daily public spectacle (Van Zoonen, 2004). More and more we witness individuals using the media precisely to push at, explore and transgress established norms of the public and private. Individuals seem to relish the potential of the media to offer the flexible tools and the free spaces within which to construct and maintain their individuality and relationships (Livingstone, 2005).

This chapter will provide a theoretical framework to examine the history, the growth and the impact of reality television on our understanding of privacy and the renegotiation of the public and/or private boundary.

REALITY TELEVISION REDEFINING CULTURE

There have been many studies examining the impact of reality television in shaping societal norms and constructs of individual viewers. According to George Gerbner's (1998, p. 6) cultural indicators model, the television content contains a common set of themes about appropriate and inappropriate social relations and behaviors that reflect cultural values and that cultivate the belief that the patterns shown are normative. Indeed the concept of "cultivation" refers to the independent contribution that television viewing makes to viewer conceptions of social reality. In the case of privacy, reality television presents us with messages regarding the appropriate or inappropriate limits and boundaries of privacy. Along with this, reality TV promises its audience revelatory insights into the lives of others as it withholds and subverts full access to it. Part of what reality TV teaches us in the early years of the new millennium is that in order to be a good citizen, we must allow ourselves to be watched as we watch those around us (Murray & Oullette, 2004, p. 4).

However, this does not imply a one-way flow of images and messages but rather a dynamic interaction between the viewer and the program being viewed. Cultivation is part of a continual, dynamic, ongoing process of interaction among messages and contexts, exchanged between the viewers and what is being viewed. Furthermore, it appears that people are more likely to respond to themes and messages that are relevant to their everyday lives or are perceived as highly realistic, a process described as *resonance*. Thus, when TV programs resonate with viewers' everyday lives, as in reality TV programming, they have a double impact (Gerbner, et al., 1986; Gerbner, 1998).

Reality TV can be viewed as what Walters (1995) calls "symptomatic text" (p. 6) as it serves as a symptom of the larger culture. In this sense, analyzing reality TV offers insight into the workings of the larger cultural context (Walters, 1995, p. 10) as reality television "reflects, rearticulates, and participates in larger cultural discourses" about "privacy, the value of privacy, and its socially acceptable manifestations" (Dubrofsky, 2011, p. 114). Reality TV thus illustrates how its participants are habituated to putting the self on public display for entertainment purposes (Dubrofsky, 2011, p. 124), and how viewers are habituated to viewing this on television.

Having said that, when it comes to social ideas and conventions about privacy in Israel, the way privacy exposure is depicted on television through the types of programming and the actions of individual actors helps shape television viewers' perceptions regarding the socially acceptable limits and boundaries of individual privacy. In the same way, the Israeli audiences' expectations of privacy tend to influence television programming, and as the increase in reality TV demonstrates, the boundaries reflecting what is considered "acceptable," both by social and broadcasting standards, and how much privacy individuals are willing to disclose are shifting every day. In Israel this shift is occurring at a faster pace than other countries, especially due to "the Big Brother phenomenon" since Israel's exposure to the "incident" between Griner and Schulberg.

We can confidently argue that reality TV is one of the most prominent TV genres of the last decade. It has become an international phenomenon and a dominant prime-time programming staple, moving from the margins of television culture to its core in dominating fashion (Hetsroni, 2011; Hill, 2005). Reality is easily monopolizing the ratings in many of the most coveted time spots (Andrejevic, 2004, p. 7). While it was initially regarded as a genre which would be a passing fad, currently the pace at which reality TV programming has spread and diversified leaves little doubt as to its reach, longevity and overall maturation into both a widely recognizable and distinct, cultural form (Murray & Oullette, 2004, pp. 1–3).

Today the fascination with what might be called the "entertaining real" (Murray and Oullette, 2009, p. 5) has led to the creation of a genre, which cuts across primetime and daytime, network and cable programming. During the 2003–2004 US Big Brother season, ten reality shows ranked among the top 25 prime-time programs in the audience-composition index for adults 18–49 with incomes of $75,000 or more. Nielsen ratings indicate that more than 18,000,000 viewers have been captivated by television programs that take ordinary people and place them in situations that have them competing in ongoing contests while being filmed 24 hours a day (Frisby, 2003).

Scholars Susan Murray and Laurie Oullette (2004) refer to reality TV as a "pervasive and provocative phenomenon"—a cultural form, an institutional and socio political development, a representational practice and a source of meaning and pleasure that is "remaking television culture" (p. 1). With its celebration of the "real" the rapid proliferation of reality TV has prompted much scholarship into the genre and its social and cultural implications. Key areas of study to date have focused on reality television's association with documentary (Friedman, 2002), its role in today's surveillance culture (Andrejevic, 2004), the relations between the genre and everyday life and the private and public spheres (van Zoonen, 2004).

This chapter focuses on the latter, on the role that reality television programs play in helping viewers to negotiate the social, political and technological forces that shape their lives—most importantly, on how reality television is both reflecting and shaping individuals' perceptions of the boundaries between the private and the public.

The premier of the reality television program *Survivor* in 2000 is considered by many to be what catapulted the genre into the public consciousness. The show, introduced by CBS, featured 16 non actors living on a small island in the South China Sea for 39 days, with one being eliminated and leaving the island every third day. Victory—in the form of one million dollars—would go to the last remaining person. The success of Survivor proved to the business and advertising community that the genre could be potentially "the next best thing," that will work. By 2002, reality TV was going strong as all of the major networks had developed reality formats and the genre dominated many of the most coveted time slots (Andrejevic, 2004).

Indeed, there is obviously an enormous desire to make one's private life public, which Van Zoonen maintains stems from a nostalgic yearning for authenticity, for ties with others like oneself and for the "social legitimization of one's own private experiences" (2004, p. 20).

WHY IS REALITY TELEVISION SO POPULAR?

Studies suggest that television viewers themselves perceive reality programs to be both exhibitionistic and voyeuristic (Hill, 2005), and acknowledge that they are drawn to this voyeuristic component (Johnson-Woods, 2002). Baruh (2009) conceptualizes voyeurism as a common (and not solely sexual) pleasure derived from access to private details.

While there are many descriptions and explanations of reality TV, the common theme lies in the reality genre's professed ability to provide viewers with an unmediated, voyeuristic, and yet often playful look at the "entertainingly real." The primary selling point is the portrayal of the "authentic," and this authenticity is often equated with the degree to which the participant is actually willing, or able, to expose his private life to the viewers watching. Accordingly, partly because of electronic media, peeking curiously into the private lives of others has become a defining characteristic of contemporary society (Calvert, 2004). This has gone hand in hand with individuals voluntarily and eagerly exposing their private lives on public television, and is in turn reflected in the increasing popularity of the reality TV genre.

The voyeuristic appeal of gazing upon individuals who come from the audience is also closely linked to the reciprocity of the voyeuristic needs of television viewers and the exhibitionism of the program participants (Groombridge, 2002). Accordingly, in an era of extensive surveillance, webcams, blogs and reality television allows individuals to engage in "empowering exhibitionism" to reclaim control over the dissemination of information about themselves (Koskela, 2004, p. 199). The reciprocal relationship between the voyeur and the exhibitionist is not only because the exhibitionist needs an audience to be successful in reclaiming control over the information (Zwick & Dholakia, 2001), but is also due to the fact that the non-pathological voyeur, looking for safe ways to observe others, needs the exhibitionist. Then what reality programs do is to provide this safe, legally sanctioned (albeit a potentially less fulfilling than corporeal) venue for the voyeur to meet the exhibitor.

Yet while viewers desire the authentic, much of the entertainment derived from watching reality shows tends to come from our awareness that what we are watching is constructed and contains "fictional" elements. Indeed, as Corner contends, "viewers, participants, and producers are less invested in absolute truth . . . and are more interested in the space that exists between truth and fiction" (Murray and Oulette, 2009, p. 8). A 2005 Associated Press/ TV Guide poll revealed that 57% of viewers felt that reality TV shows showed some truth but were mostly distorted, and 25% said that they were totally made up (Murray & Oulette, 2009, p. 8).

On the other edge of the sword, the production side, reality TV programs are attractive to producers because they integrate cheap production expenses with the potential for high ratings. Additionally, there is no need for a professional script or experienced actors—this being a large attraction. A large part of many reality TV programs is based upon a vicious competition among the competitors, which then leads to high emotional levels among the viewers. As such, Neiger and Josman (2005) attribute the reality programs' success to the illusion of democratic participation and to their ability to create an image of a pluralistic sphere that ostensibly lends greater power both to the audience and to the participants (Murray & Oulette, 2004). Viewers can promote or remove competitors and can easily—just by clicking an Internet site or by sending a text message—influence which ousted competitors can be brought back. On the surface, the power is in the hands of the public who are able to determine the final outcomes, the winners and the losers.

HOW BIG BROTHER IS REDEFINING PRIVACY

The way in which privacy is portrayed in reality television sends important messages to viewers regarding the value of not only privacy but also surveillance and the socially acceptable and appropriate ratio between the private and the public sphere. This in turn works to reflect social conceptions of privacy as well as the scope of the right to privacy, based upon social codes and conventions (Lavie-Dinur & Karniel, 2008).

Reality TV is presented as a more "authentic" reflection of real life. This is in contrast to the drama genre that has actors and scripts. Thus, we argue that the types of privacy exposure depicted in reality programming play a more significant role in how viewers interpret and define the boundaries of privacy exposure. As Murray and Oullette (2004) write, "Our exposure to ordinary people's willingness to live their lives in front of cameras makes us "normalize" this phenomenon and in turn opens us to the possibility of even participating in it (p. 9).

The yearly escalation of reality programs may imply a greater legitimization and indifference toward the phenomenon of "Big Brother." This program has reshaped the concept of privacy in Israeli and in worldwide culture. The Big Brother's appeal lies, in part, in its ability to provide audiences around the world with a "highly artificial, but trustworthily transparent vehicle to observe and participate in human emotions, stratagems, characters and relationships as they unfold in a domestic setting" (Hartley, 2004, p. 309).

Big Brother has gained high international marketing success (Frau-Meigs, 2006). It became one of the Netherlands top-rated shows within a month, drawing 15 million viewers for its climax on New Year's Eve 1999 (Hill, 2005, p. 5). In 2002, the popular format was adapted to the United States under the simple premise: "Ten people. No privacy. Three months. No outside contact" (Wilson, 2004, p. 325). Ten individuals were chosen to participate in the show's first season; the group would live together in a house, surrounded by video cameras recording their every move, every two weeks a contestant would be voted off, with the last remaining contestant winning a grand prize of $500,000.

The Big Brother format includes a Spartan house and living style, a long period of confinement, no access to mass media, constant surveillance, participating in regular "confessions," various tasks/tests, the constant threat of being ousted and the nuances and dramas of everyday reality. Every room (including the bathroom) in the Big Brother house is wired with remote-controlled cameras and microphones, thus leaving no space for the houseguests to escape the electronic gaze of cameras. Even when the lights are turned off, night vision cameras monitor all activities. In order to "spice up" the mundaneness of everyday occurrences, producers assign participants daily and weekly challenges which result in either prizes or penalties.

Moreover, the only place for participants to escape each other is a closet-sized room, painted entirely red, where they can speak directly to the show's producers, who refer to themselves collectively as the "Big Brother." It is in the Red Room that the houseguests are free to speak candidly about the other participants and about themselves and be interrogated by the producers about specific conflicts or situations occurring in the house.

The format is based upon cross-cultural principles, thus explaining the large number of adaptations of the show around the world. In Orwell's book, *1984*, from which the show Big Brother takes its name, the loss of privacy is perceived as a disaster of an inhuman and totalitarian society. The book portrays a world in which there is no privacy, telling the story of a man who succumbs to the power of Big Brother, which is actually a TV set with a dark, totalitarian mechanism operating it. The book presents a world in which surveillance is imposed on people against their will. Instead the Big Brother show focuses on individuals who voluntarily sign up to have their lives monitored and on display for the world to see. According to Dorfman (2002), the program was first created in the Netherlands where at present the name represents, though with an iota of irony, a democratic experience; a free and intensifying one derived from the participants' consent to be placed under 24/7 surveillance.

In spite of the conditions described above, young people, from all over the world, fight for the opportunity to participate in the Big Brother program, as exemplified by the Israeli case, and are prepared and excited to sacrifice their privacy for the chance of fame. The popularity of the show thus offers a re formulation of George Orwell's famous phrase: No longer is Big Brother ominously watching. Rather, millions of people are watching Big Brother: surveillance itself has become a mediated spectacle (Andrejevic, 2004).

Big Brother has a unique place in the history of international television; it seems more than any other format to have become the object of intense social criticism. Indeed, Ernest Mathijs (2002) has observed that the reception of the first Big Brother series in Europe provoked wide-scale debates, including vehement reactions of public revulsion and moral anxiety by academics, opinion makers, politicians and moral guardians. The program has been openly denounced for its debasement of quality and privacy, with policy makers even threatening to ban the program in certain countries. Many scholars criticize the show for providing "low-brow" entertainment and for its connection with the "peeping tom" syndrome. Journalists, psychologists, opinion leaders, and commentators "condemning the show as an inhumane experiment, bordering on the bizarre ad the unacceptable, exploiting voyeurism and invading personal privacy" (Mathijs, 2002, p. 10).

This house offers a wide range of options available to participants with regard to how they present themselves. The self can be put on display in various modes of affection, solidarity, insincerity, confrontation, and downright aggression. Accordingly, the first to be ousted from the program will be accused of not acting "sincerely" enough and not being "real."

BIG BROTHER IN ISRAEL: A CASE STUDY

The Big Brother program quickly became very popular among Israel audience. The program, which was first broadcast in 2008, continues to be the most popular reality program in the country. It captivated audience's attention and quickly became the subject of public and private discussion. It has broadcasted every summer since 2008 and even the "Tzuk Eitan" (Operation Protective Edge) war in the summer of 2014 did not stop the program from broadcasting. Indeed, until 2013, 32% of Israeli teenagers said they would be interested in auditioning for the program, while 47% think the show reflects the social reality of the country (Barak, 2012). The program is broadcast on

Channel 2 (for free) and Channel 20 (for purchase) for an approximate time period of 100 days and includes approximately 32 episodes.

The house residents are required to stay in the Big Brother's house for the entire duration of the program. There are cameras in every room of the house, and they are always turned on. The winner, who "survives" all the "evictions" by residents and audience, is rewarded a 1,000,000 NIS prize (equivalent to approximately $300,000). The show's popularity in Israel is exemplified by the fact that the first episode of the current 2015 V.I.P season, had over 1.14 million viewers (Toker, 2013), reaching a 40% rating, compared to only 2% during the opening of the US version (Alper, 2015).

THE NATURE OF EXPOSURE ON BIG BROTHER: THE FIRST BIG BROTHER SEASON AS A CASE STUDY

Using the privacy typology, we conducted a quantitative and qualitative study on the first season of Big Brother (broadcast in 2008) in Israel in order to examine the type and degree of privacy exposure on the show. The show featured sixteen housemates (another four joined 56 days later) who agreed to live together, under constant surveillance, in a suburban Jerusalem house for the chance to win one million shekels (the equivalent of approximately $260,000). In addition to the show's main broadcast on Israel's National Channel 2, there was a 24-hour live broadcast on HOT, an Israeli cable channel, as well as on the Internet. Thus, we analyzed all the 32 Big Brother episodes aired on Channel 2 and additionally seven random broadcast hours on Channel 20 (cable TV). Internet viewers could choose which camera images they wanted to view, while HOT viewers could only see camera images chosen by the Big Brother staff. The house was equipped with 50 surveillance cameras, which were operated by the Big Brother in-house staff.

PRIVACY TYPOLOGY

- Factual (Personal) Exposure: Refers to personal information and data, such as marital status, financial status, health condition, educational background, employment history as well as biometric information and data, fingerprints, retinal scans, facial structure recognition and genetic information.
- Visual Exposure: Emphasizes physical representation by means of photographs, revealing pictures of the body, video clips and so forth.
- Exposure of Identity and Emotions: Outlines information about private opinions, viewpoints, feelings, principles, religious beliefs and personal characteristics.

- Exposure of Preferences: Individual consumer habits and preferences are under discussion in this realm (with regard to merchandise, food, and more.)

We examined the participants' privacy exposure according to level of familiarity existing between individuals:

- Level 1, Basic Familiarity: This level of exposure refers to basic information revealed during the initial introduction between two people. For example, details about ones place of residence, nationality and hobbies, among others.
- Level 2, Medium Familiarity: This level refers to information revealed between two personal acquaintances consistently over time. This includes references to the person's family, mood exposure and others.
- Level 3, High Familiarity: This refers to the type of information revealed between close friends and family, individuals with a high level of familiarity between one another. It is defined by relatively high exposure of emotional and personal information, that is, intimate details, and the like. It refers to behavior patterns that exist in the private sphere.
- Level 4, Intimate Familiarity: This level refers to the type of exposure that predominantly often occurs between spouses. This exposure level refers to behavior of a sexual nature and relates to levels of emotional exposure and behavioral patterns generally relegated to the private sphere.

Once all the relevant variables were collected, we calculated the exposure averages regarding each participant. These averages were added up according to the exposure-level indexes (as above mentioned). The exposure levels were used to help calculate correlations between levels of exposure and the participant's level of success in the program. Success was measured according to how many episodes the participant was featured in (before being eliminated from the show).

RESULTS

At first, the main types of participant exposure were examined (an average of each episode). This was done in order to understand the exact characteristics of exposure and the extent of privacy concession as they actually took place in the program.

Figure 3.1 reveals the various exposure types, according to their relative frequency, that occurred on average in each episode. As can be seen from the data, the main exposure types were clearly physical (cleavage, short/tight clothing, and the like). A much smaller fragment of exposure referred to

Channel

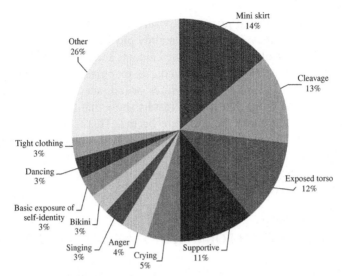

Figure 3.1   **Exposure Types on Channel 2.**

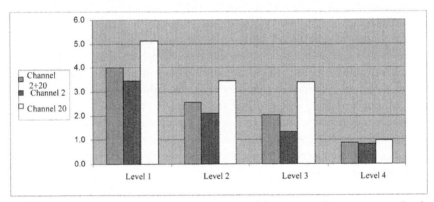

Figure 3.2   **Exposure averages per episode per participant according to exposure levels and channels.**

emotional exposure (crying, anger, among others). Participants rarely engaged in aspects of exposure such as factual exposure and distinct sexual behavior.

Levels of Familiarity

The findings reveal that the higher the level of exposure (in terms of familiarity) the rarer it is. In other words, intimate behavior or exposure of intimate details were relatively rare while exposure of less intimate details and less intimate behaviors (as one would share with strangers, acquaintances) were more frequently seen on screen.

The findings reveal that privacy exposure on Big Brother has limitations and clear characteristics. Exposure is mainly physical and includes exposure of present behavior of one's body. The cameras see everything: body, body language, exposed body parts, and of course, external behavior. On the contrary, there are very few factual exposures or intimate stories that have hidden details. Furthermore, the study's results show that the more intense the exposure is, the less often the exposure occurs. This is almost self-evident but seems to confirm that defending privacy is still considered valuable and significant. The Big Brother program features many instances of level 1 and level 2 privacy exposure, whereas high levels of exposure of couples' intimate relations are relatively rare.

INTERVIEWS WITH FORMER REALITY TV PARTICIPANTS

As a follow-up to this study, with the aim of gaining additional insights into the abovementioned findings, we interviewed former reality TV show participants in order to understand the significance of their exposure on the show in retrospect.

We conducted interviews with a number of different Israeli reality TV participants in order to understand the ways in which they negotiated the boundaries and limits of their privacy during their time on these shows. Most of the participants remarked that they chose to participate in these shows for the "experience" and indicated that they strove to be "real" throughout the entire filming. In the words of one of the participants on the show, "I knew I had nothing to hide. What's to hide? My weaknesses and my strengths are human, and I cannot treat them as non-existent. So I have nothing to hide. And that is part of the experience."

Others indicated that they had a personal strategy of what to reveal about themselves and what not to. As one participant stated, "I made the decision not to reveal things in my personal life, family." Another participant exclaimed, "I thought I would be myself, and spare the camera any negative things about me, but of course you cannot hide anything from the camera. Yet I still clung to myself as I progressed." These statements emphasize the difficulty that arose among participants in Big Brother Israel when attempting to control which parts of their intimate selves they were willing to disclose. As one participant put it, "The question becomes how you handle the situation itself. You can try to be emotionally distant, but there are certain situations when you cannot." Indeed, another participant confessed that although he made a conscious effort to maintain his composure and keep his personal thoughts and feelings to himself, "there were moments when I broke down and collapsed."

For many, the invasion of privacy was daunting and some even labeled it as a "traumatizing" experience. According to one participant, "The experience was very difficult, and you do not understand right away just how difficult the invasion of privacy is. On a daily basis you are being filmed 24 hours a day." However, when asked about whether they had been concerned about the loss of privacy before the show, the responses were mixed, with some participants claiming that, "there were many things I decided not to disclose in order to protect my family's privacy. So I did not share many details about my personal life," and others admitting, "To be honest, I didn't even think about it," and "I got used to it [the loss of privacy] almost completely. I even enjoyed it."

These interviews provided us with the first indication that participants on reality television programs, as outlined by the Israeli case, go through a complex process of deciding which aspects of their personal lives they wish to expose on public television. Considering their thoughts we can identify a complex understanding of the border between public and private and—that is, how this distinction is being blurred episode after episode.

BIG BROTHER ISRAEL: SEASON SIX

The sixth season of Big Brother Israel ended on August 2014. In view of the findings from the first season, which arguably had a more innocent nature, we decided to explore whether the six-year difference between the first and sixth seasons had increased the level of participants' privacy exposure on the show.

We can unequivocally state that by season six, the degree of participants' exposure had increased in each of the parameters examined. Season six featured a love triangle between one man and two women, incidents of physical and verbal abuse, exhibitionism that bordered on pornography, and frequent outbursts of tears, arguments and shouting matches. To illustrate the exposure that characterized season six, we analyzed several prominent examples involving the four finalists, using the exposure measures we developed.

Factual Exposure in Big Brother Israel, Season Six

The season six winner was Tal Gilboa, who joined the house and the program as an ideological campaigner of veganism. On the show, Tal was represented as a determined, aggressive, contentious woman who consistently expressed her values. She devoted her life to veganism; her body was adorned with tattoos of vegan-related texts, and she frequently repeated the catch phrase that she would "fight for her truth" (her truth being opposition to the cruel killing of animals for food). In addition to her ideology, and more than any other participant, Tal expansively recounted the details of her private life and her past. She spoke of her three daughters, her husband, and her difficult childhood. Her divorced parents had been inadequate caregivers and she had been passed back and forth between her mother and father. In one episode where the residents took turns exhibiting their talents, the group's oldest woman, Martine Sollel, chose to impersonate the other participants in a story-like fashion. When she described Tal, she told a story about "Kitzenet" [a made-up name based on the root of the word "extreme" in Hebrew], a woman who defended extreme opinions because she had been neglected by her parents in her childhood. Tal's reaction to Sollel's presentation was a combination of anger and tears, and when she was confronted, Tal argued that she was the only one who was permitted to reveal and discuss her childhood or define herself as an abandoned child, adding, "I never took into account this crazy level of personal exposure."

The mirror that was held up to her, based on the facts that she herself had disclosed over the course of the season, and especially the interpretation that was given to these facts, was a turning point in her understanding of the enormous gap that had emerged between her exposure during the season and her desire to protect her privacy or at least her desire to control the interpretation of the facts relating to her life. The contrast between her conscious desire for publicity for an ideological cause and her effective public exposure highlighted her situation: we want to reveal ourselves and gain exposure, retaining control over the messages we convey and their intensity, but we do not always comprehend the price of that exposure. As seen by this Israeli example, Tal had willingly shared details of her private life, her thoughts, her emotions, and of course, information on the food she buys and consumes. Throughout season six, Tal wanted to be part of the group in the house; she sought out interactions with the other participants and was specifically interested in becoming visible to the viewer audience—yet at the same time, she wanted to protect her privacy. This outlines the gap between what we in Israel believe and what we do.

Physical Exposure in Big Brother Israel, Season Six

Season six was also characterized by significant physical exposure. Of the ten women who entered the house, five were young and physically attractive. Having packed several bathing suits with them, the young women would frequently change into their poolside attire. Internet gossip sites published numerous photos of the participants in their bathing suits, with captions such as "hot pool party." Extensive screen time was devoted to the participants cavorting in the pool, with cameras focused on their exposed bodies.

Linor Sheffer, a finalist, was the topic of lively discussions, in which she was called attractive, sexy, and a twerker. Online gossip sites called her "the sexiest participant in Big Brother's history." One of her more revealing bathing suits triggered lively discussions among house participants and on popular online media in Israel, which focused on the boundary between legitimate exposure and pornography. In this respect, season six differed significantly from season one of Big Brother, whose female participants were not especially attractive, and neither the participants nor the cameras focused on the women's bodies or on their designer swimwear. Physical exposure in season one was insignificant, and specifically participants in bikinis accounted for a mere 3% of the total airtime.

Emotional Exposure in Big Brother Israel, Season 6

Season six was characterized by emotional bouts of crying, shouting, arguments, and even physical abuse. In this season, Linor Sheffer and Tal Gilboah maintained an increasingly tense relationship. In one of their arguments, Tal, after having been provoked by Linor during dinner, poured a glass of wine on Linor in order to force her to stop speaking. Her act triggered intense reactions from the other participants, who were sharply divided in supporting or opposing the act. Tal was summoned to the Big Brother room and was reprimanded on screen for her violent and inappropriate behavior, the keynote being that: on screen. Again we see how privacy is reduced and the line between the public and private sphere is becoming blurred within the Israeli context. Several days later, Linor walked up to Tal and poured a glass of wine over her, which she justified as an effort to recover her lost respect, signaling that she was not the kind of person to acquiesce when she was the object of violence. The sight of the foul-mouthed and abusive conduct of these two strong-willed women constituted the peak of this type of verbal violence.

In contrast, in season one, no physical signs of affection between the participants were caught on camera, and the audience was only privy to hints of season winner Shifra Cornfeld's crush on Tzabar Gadish—but this was a story of unrequited love that remained one sided until the end of the season. In season one, participants showed more emotional restraint and refrained from outward displays of affection and emotion.

SUMMARY

The time that elapsed between season one and season six was also reflected in the differences in participants' conduct in the house. Participants' exposure increased steadily from one season to the next, and the audience became accustomed to the increasing levels of exposure, and accepting it as an ordinary aspect of reality TV that takes place in front of cameras.

Like season one, season six was very popular, with an average rating of 40%, compared to just 2% for the US version of Big Brother during this time. Thousands of Israelis showed up to audition for the show. They came to talk about themselves, and reveal and share information about themselves; they came to gain fame through a "significant experience" or to convey an ideological message. By coming to the auditions, they discounted what might previously have been considered a high value: their privacy. In effect, they did much more than waive their privacy, because what they sought was not merely to become famous but also to make their presence known. They auditioned for the show with the intention of becoming observed, recognized and loved. These are all outcomes, which they expected to be a source of enjoyment. Any assumption that participants would restrain their behavior because they were being monitored was proved wrong.

From season one to season six, participants in the house freely and openly discussed their lives, revealed their bodies, fell in love and had sexual intercourse in front of the cameras. Ironically, to succeed on the show, participants had to show their "genuine" and "authentic" selves. They were told that their popularity was contingent on their ability to act authentically and naturally in public, as if they were in the privacy of their own home.

The blurring of the public and private boundary, and the increasing relinquishment of privacy prompted by reality TV has become heightened by the emergence of social networks, the blogosphere, Instagram and WhatsApp, among others. The proliferation of mobile phones has made it possible for the private to invade the public space without warning. Furthermore, reinforcing the desire to waive one's privacy and consciously seek admiration and love, and to accumulate "likes" (as will be demonstrated in the upcoming chapters.

REFERENCES

Alper, R. (2015, May 13). Israel's specific degenerative disease. *Haaretz Online*. [Hebrew]. Retrieved from: http://www.haaretz.co.il/gallery/television/tv-review/.premium-1.2635321.

Andrejevic, M. (2004). *Reality TV: The work of being watched*. Lanham, Maryland: Rowman & Littlefield Publishers.

Barak, R. (2012, March 3). 74% of youth: The reality affects our behavior. *Globes*. [Hebrew]. Retrieved from: http://www.globes.co.il/news/article.aspx?did=1000730855.

Baruh, L. (2009). Publicized intimacies on reality television: An analysis of voyeuristic content and its contribution to the appeal of reality programming. *Journal of Broadcasting & Electronic Media, 53*(2), 190–210. doi:10.1080/08838150902907678.

Choi, H. (2015). White men still dominate reality television: Discriminatory casting and the need for regulation. *Communications and Entertainment Law Journal, 37*, 163–163.

Calvert, C. (2004). Revisiting the voyeurism value in the first amendment: From the sexually sordid to the details of death. *The Seattle University Law Review, 27*, 721.

Dorfman, R. (2002). The future of reality . . . television. *EXQUISITE CORPSE*. www.copse.org. Spring/Summer Issue.

Dubrofsky, R.E. (2011). Surveillance on reality television and Facebook: From authenticity to flowing data. *Communication Theory, 21*(2), 111–129.

Frau-Meigs, D. (2006). Big brother and reality TV in Europe: Towards a theory of situated acculturation by the media. *European Journal of Communication, 1/21*, 33–56.

Friedman, J. (Ed.) (2002). *Reality squared: Televisual discourse on the real*. New Brunswick, NJ: Rutgers University Press.

Friedman, M. (2015). *Survivor* skills: Authenticity, representation and why I want to teach reality TV. *Dialogue: The Interdisciplinary Journal of Popular Culture and Pedagogy, 2*(1).

Frisby, C. (2003). *Reality television has positive impact on viewers*. Columbia: University of Missouri.

Gerbner, G. (1998). Cultivation analysis: An overview. *Mass Communication & Society* I, 3/4, 175–195.

Gerbner, G., Gross, L, Morgan, M., & Signorielli, N. (1986). Living with television: The dynamics of the cultivation process. In J. Bryant & D. Zillman (Eds.), *Perspectives on media effects* (pp. 17–40). Hillsdale, NJ: Lawrence Erlbaum Associates.

Groombridge, N. (2002). Crime control or crime culture TV? *Surveillance & Society, 1*(1), 30–46.

Hill, A. (2005). *Reality TV: Audiences and popular factual television*. New York: Routledge.

Hartley, J. (2004). Kiss me Kat: Shakespeare, big brother, and the taming of the self. In S. Murray & L. Oullette (Eds.). *Reality TV: Remaking television culture* (pp. 303–322). New York: New York University Press.

Hetsroni, A. (Ed.) (2011). *Reality television: Merging the global and the local*. Hauppauge, NY: Nova Science Publishers.

Johansson, S. (2015). Celebrity culture and audiences: a Swedish case study. *Celebrity Studies*, (ahead-of-print), 1–15.

Johnson-Woods, T. (2002). *Big Bother: Why did that reality TV show become such a phenomenon?* St. Lucia, Queensland, Australia: University of Queensland Press.

Koskela, H. (2004). Webcams, TV shows and mobile phones: Empowering exhibitionism. *Surveillance & Society, 2*(2/3), 199–215.

Kraft, D. (2008, December 16). Culture wars emerge around Israeli 'Big Brother'. Retrieved from http://www.jta.org/2008/12/16/arts-entertainment/culture-wars-emerge-around-israeli-big-brother on May 22, 2015.

Lavie-Dinur, A., & Karniel, Y. (2013). 'Esti Ha'mechoeret': Ugly Esti. In J. McCabe & K. Akass (Eds.), *TV's Betty goes global: From telenovela to international brand*. (167–173). London, UK: I.B. Tauris.

Lavie-Dinur, A., & Karniel, Y. (2008). Sacrificing privacy for the sake of fame: How television is going to erode privacy in Israel. Exploration in Media Ecology (EME), *The Journal of Media Ecology Association, 7,* 255–269.

Livingstone, S. (2005). Chapter 7: In defence of privacy: Mediating the public/private boundary at home. In *Changing media, changing Europe* (pp. 163–185). Bristol, UK: Intellect Ltd.

Marcus, S. (2015). Celebrity, past and present. *Public Culture, 27*(1), 1–5.

Mathijs, E. (2002). Big brother and critical discourse. *Television and new media, 3*(3), 311–322.

Mendick, H., Allen, K., & Harvey, L. (2015). 'We can get everything we want if we try hard': Young people, celebrity, hard work. *British Journal of Educational Studies, 63*(2), 161–178.

Murray, S., & Ouellette, L. (2004). *Reality TV: Remaking television culture.* New York: New York University Press.

Neiger, M., & Josman, A. (2005). *The illusion of democratic choice: How reality shows obtain audience cooperation.* Tel Aviv: Haim Herzog Institute, Tel-Aviv University. (40 pp.). [Research paper in Hebrew].

Orwell, G. (1948). *1984.* Penguin Books: London.

Tal-Or, N., & Hershman-Shitrit, M. (2015). Self-Disclosure and the liking of participants in reality TV. *Human Communication Research, 41*: 245–267.

Toker, N. (2013, May 23). Reality TV took over Israel. *The Marker.* [Hebrew] Retrieved from: http://www.themarker.com/advertising/1.2027656

Toker, N. (2013, May 11). Big brother again: 1.14 million viewers in the opening chapter of "Big Brother" VIP. [Hebrew]. Retrieved from: http://www.themarker.com/advertising/1.2633806.

Van Zoonen, L. (2004). Desire and resistance: Big brother in the Dutch public sphere. In E. Mathijs & J. Jones (Eds.), *Big Brother international: Formats, critics and publics,* (16–24). London and New York: Wallflower Press.

Walters, S.D. (1995). *Material girls: Making sense of feminist cultural theory.* Berkeley: University of Press.

Zwick, D., & Dholakia, N. (2001). Contrasting European and American approaches to privacy in electronic markets: Property right versus civil right. *Electronic Markets, 11*(2), 116–120.

Chapter 4

Getting the "Like"

Facebook

On July 2, 2014, Facebook's second most powerful executive, Sheryl Sandberg, apologized for conducting secret psychological tests on approximately 700,000 Facebook users in 2012. The experiment, which was revealed by a scientific paper published in the March issue of Proceedings of National Academy of Sciences, aimed to see whether positive and/or negative words in messages would lead to positive and/or negative content in status updates, that is, an "emotional contagion" across the social network (Preston, 2014). Facebook not only faced legal repercussions but also faced stern criticism over its handling of the experiment which was not explained to users and therefore was performed without their consent. On that note, some researchers and commentators referred to this action as "creepy," "evil," "terrifying" and even "super disturbing" (Gibbs, 2014). Facebook has insisted that the experiment was covered by its terms of service (Preston, 2014). Sandberg, in response to the outcry, said, "We take privacy and security at Facebook really seriously because that is something that allows people to share opinions and emotions" (Preston, 2014).

The public outcry over Facebook's "emotional contagion" experiment comes after years of criticism surrounding the social network's data collection practices and its frequent changes to its privacy policy ("Facebook Data Policy," 2015). Indeed, with almost every new product launch (or acquisition, such as Instagram), Facebook alters its privacy settings, often using confusing and complicated language that many users claim is difficult to understand. The result has been public outcry by both individuals and privacy groups. In tandem, Facebook has been subject to a wave of lawsuits, including a $20 million settlement the company had to pay for giving away users' personal information (Kleinman, 2014). Yet the obscure and complicated language surrounding privacy reflected Facebook CEO Mark Zuckerberg's view on the subject. Zuckerberg has been quoted saying he doesn't believe in privacy and that privacy is no longer a social norm (Oremus, 2014). This was perhaps best indicated in the company's "public by default" policy, where the default setting was that all posts were made publicly visible (Cashmore, 2010).

However, things may be changing. In May 2014, Facebook rolled out a series of privacy features and private services such as messaging and anonymous logins to better clarify its privacy policy and protect users' privacy. Possibly the most significant change was that it changed the default audience for new members' posts from "public" to "friends". According to Slate Magazine's Will Oremus (2014), "Privacy is as hot today in the technology industry as 'sharing' and 'openness' were four years ago. And Facebook intends to capitalize on it."

When asked about this new strategic shift toward privacy, Zuckerberg responded: "One of the things that we focus on the most is creating private spaces for people to share things and have interactions that they couldn't have had elsewhere. So we're looking for new opportunities to create new dynamics like that and open up new, different private spaces for people where they can then feel comfortable sharing and having the freedom to express something to people that they otherwise wouldn't be able to" (Oremus, 2014).

Zuckerberg believes that privacy is about control: "What people want isn't complete privacy. It isn't that they want secrecy. It's that they want control over what they share and what they don't" (Zimmer, 2014). In regard to the post about privacy changes, Facebook said, "We recognize that it is much worse for someone to accidentally share with everyone when they actually meant to share just with friends, compared with the reverse."

Thus, in a world where norms and expectations about privacy and control are constantly shifting—how are users negotiating their privacy expectations and exposure across social media networks?

INTRODUCTION

The increasing popularity of Online Social Networks, especially Facebook, is challenging our traditional notions and expectations of privacy due to the relative ease with which personal information about ourselves and others is published, shared and accessed (Buchanan, Paine, Joinson, & Reips, 2007; DeCew, 1997, p. 145; Katsh, 1989). The root motivations for site members are often communication, information exchange and maintaining social relationships (Levin & Sanchez-Abril, 2009). In conjunction with the prior notion, several studies recognize both self-disclosure (Acquisti & Gross, 2006; Debatin, Lovejoy, Horn, & Hughes, 2009; Nosko, Wood, & Molema, 2010; Schrammel, Kiffel, & Tscheligi, 2009) and social connections

(Brandtzaeg, Luders, & Sjetke, 2010; Ellison, Heino, & Gibbs, 2006; Zweir, Araujo, Boukes, & Willemsen 2011) as core behaviors on social networks.

However, while the benefits of OSN's include socializing, redefining the self, and networking, it is often the case that in order to reap these benefits of socializing and making new friends, individuals must disclose information about themselves that would normally be part of a gradual "getting-to-know-you" process *offline* (name, school, personal interests, and more) (Lenhart & Madden, 2007, p. 6). Yet, when it comes to social network sites, this kind of information is disclosed *online*—with individuals often posting intimate photos of themselves and their peers, blogging about relationships, venting about bosses and colleagues online, among other activities that are traditionally deemed private (Levin & Sánchez, 2009). Indeed, certain social mechanisms at play often reward the disclosure of information and entice users to share more information (Bronstein, 2014; Schrammel, Kiffel, & Tscheligi, 2009). According to Charles Fried (1970), privacy may be conceptualized as a form of social currency. Sharing private information, he argued, forms the basis for intimate relationships of friendship, love, trust and relationships that often take years to develop. This is echoed by Christofides, Muise and Desmarais (2009) who observed that there is a reciprocal relationship between trust and self-disclosure in online communication. They found that "information disclosure increases the impression of trustworthiness and results in recipro-cal information disclosure on the part of the conversation partner" (p. 342). However, OSN's have loosened traditional notions of intimacy and friend-ship as many online socializers post personal information on OSNs and thus make it available to a large audience of "friends," seemingly without much concern over the loss of control (Levin & Sanchez-Abril, 2009) regarding their privacy.

Users of social networking websites tend to disclose much personal infor-mation online, but they still seem to retain an expectation of privacy. Using the privacy exposure typology developed in previous chapters, this chapter aims to uncover the aspects of personal information that users are more will-ing to disclose and what they opt to retain control over. This typology draws on Nissenbaum's theory of contextual integrity, which is based on a pluralis-tic concept of privacy. Specifically, Nissenbaum's theory claims that privacy is contextually defined, meaning that conceptions of privacy vary across con-texts. According to Nissenbaum (and other contextual approaches), there is no clearly defined public/private distinction, but rather privacy expectations are viewed as the negotiated information norms within a particular commu-nity or situation (Martin, 2012). Thus, our privacy typology is a tool to better understand the different ways individuals negotiate their privacy expectations across different contexts. This chapter attempts to draw a new map to con-front the issue of privacy in the new media age.

ONLINE PRIVACY

The issue of online privacy is relevant to almost every Internet user. It is raised time and time again on the media and public agenda and motivates discussions of the public's right to privacy. In the context of new media, the focus is mainly on what information is obtained about individuals and how this information is used. This topic is known as "information privacy" or "data protection" as it is called in Europe (Birnhack & Elkin-Koren, 2009, p. 5). The debate about online privacy takes place between consumers on the one hand, and websites and online commercial bodies and companies on the other. It focuses mainly on the notion of consent. In other words, privacy is violated in the absence of the consumer's informed consent with respect to receipt or disclosure of certain types of information (Yael Onn et al., 2005). Such informed consent is related to two major values of information privacy: the right to control information and the right to prevent access (Birnhack & Elkin-Koren, 2009, p. 7).

According to Onn (2005), the right to privacy grants us the ability to decide "which parts of this personal space can be accessed by others and to control the extent, manner and timing for using those parts we decided to expose" (p. 26). The uproar of public and media discourse regarding violations of privacy without explicit user consent sometimes leads to policy changes on the part of the violating website. This has primarily been the case with Facebook, whose immense popularity has placed it in the limelight of public discourse concerning privacy over the past two years. Violation of online privacy sometimes creates what Michael Birnhack and Niva Elkin-Koren (2009) have termed "privacy events," patterned on the term "media events." Such events cause the use of a particular website to decline (2010, pp. 10–11). This potentially results in boycotting certain products, as in the case of Buzz, the social network launched by Google. Complaints from Gmail users that Buzz had violated their privacy by automatically and without permission connecting them to its service led Google to apologize and to change its privacy settings (Dickter, 2010). From that point on, there would no longer be an "auto-connect" to the social network, but rather an "auto-suggest," enabling users to decide whether or not to accept the suggestion.

According to Levine and Sanchez-Abril (2009), individuals who socialize online have developed a new notion of what they deem as privacy, which takes into account not only user control over privacy but also protection of their dignity and reputation. They call this notion network privacy. This dignity-focused notion of privacy emphasizes the development of one's personality, reputation, inner self and the ability to construct different "situational personalities" (p. 1013). According to network privacy, "information is considered by online socializers to be private as long as it is not disclosed outside of the network to which they initially disclosed it, if it originates with them, or as long as it does not affect their established online personae, if it originates with others" (p. 1002). In short, network privacy is based on the "expected accessibility of personal information to social constituencies." Thus, Levin and Sanchez-Abril (2009) argue that when online socializers feel a threat to their privacy, it is really their reputation, dignity, persona or online identity that feels threatened. Their study's findings reveal that many online socializers post personal information seemingly without much concern over the loss of control, yet react with indignation when their personal information is accessed, used, or disclosed by individuals perceived to be outside of their social network (Levin & Sanchez-Abril, 2009).

This notion of privacy represents a much more fluid and comprehensive definition in regard to changing privacy norms and expectations among online social network users. Along with the notion of online privacy, it is essential to understand the legal differences between America and Europe as this right to be forgotten stems from an important ongoing debate encapsulating the book's privacy argument. The American and European legal approaches to informational privacy differ quite significantly. Where as in the United States the legal discussion is focused mainly on regulating data that is collected by the federal government, the European legislation has led to a set of comprehensive omnibus policies on the treatment of personal information, without regard to the controllers of the data, be it is public or private (Stratford & Stratford, 1998).

In the United States there is no single law that provides a comprehensive treatment of data protection or privacy issues. The legal tradition therefore consists of constitutional interpretations provided by courts, and a number of laws and executive orders addressing different privacy-intrusion cases separately, as illustrated by Stratford and Stratford (1998), where personal data by the census or national health services is used.

In contrast, the European institutions have established major comprehensive legal policies covering the issue of privacy as a whole. Embedded in its comprehensive convention on human rights, the European Convention of Human Rights 1950 (ECHR), Article 8 recognizes one's right to "private and family life, his home and his correspondence". This is viewed as one of the fundamental human rights. Furthermore, this guarantees that "there shall be no interference by a public authority with the exercise of this right" subject to specific exceptions of national interests under which restrictions of the right are permitted, such as public's security and safety or the protection of the rights of others" (EHCR, Article 8).

Moreover, the European court of human rights has clarified in various rulings that Article 8 not only obliged states to refrain from any actions that violate the rights, but that they were in certain circumstances also under positive obligations to actively secure effective respect for private life (Handbook on European Data Protection Law, 2014). In 1981, with the emergence of information technology and collection of personal data, and the need to reinforce the protection of privacy in the digital area, Convention 108 for the protection of individuals with regard to the automatic processing of personal data was opened for signature. This applied to all data processing carried out by both the private and the public sectors. The convention also declares the individual's right to know that stored information about him/her, and more importantly to correct it, if justified.

A striking example of the tension between the development of new information and big data technologies, and privacy-related issues, and European influence in that field, is the recent-evolving notion of "the right to be forgotten." This has become a central issue among agencies and scholars addressing the topic of privacy in the digital age. The principle underpinning the discussion over that notion is the individual's right to decide what happens with the information on their matter (Bennett, 2012), which is in accord with Westin's definitions of privacy.

The concept of the right to be forgotten is specifically mentioned and broadly described in the European proposal for a general data protection regulation released in 2012, and aimed at modernizing the existing directive and incorporating aspects of technological advances (Bennett, 2012; Rosen, 2012). It is described as the right of individuals to "have their data fully removed when it is no longer needed for the purposes for which it was collected," specifically pointing to social networking sites information, such as profiles and photos. This reform is currently still under negotiation (Fact Sheet on the "Right to be Forgotten," 2014).

On May 2014, the "right to be forgotten" was also incorporated into a landmark ruling by the court of justice of the European union (Travis & Arthur, 2014). The case involved a Spanish man who complained that an auction notice of his home on Google's search engine violated his privacy rights. The complainant's financial difficulties have been resolved for years but the newspaper records kept showing up when clicking his name on Google. The EU court has ruled that individuals have the right, under certain conditions, to ask search engines to remove links with personal information about them, if requested (Toobin, 2014). Not surprisingly, the ruling has resulted in a controversy over the implications of such a right, primarily, its conflict with the right to freedom of speech.

ONLINE SOCIAL NETWORKS

In recent years, we have witnessed the rapid proliferation of a new class of information technologies, commonly known as social media, and specifically

OSN, which facilitate and encourage interpersonal communication and collaboration using Internet-based platforms (Kane et al., 2014). Among the best known of these tools are sites such as Facebook, LinkedIn and Twitter, each of which have enjoyed mass adoption and are used by hundreds of millions of people as of this writing. These sites have gained traction in every facet of the public and private arena (Dubrofsky, 2011, p. 115), as well as much attention from scholars (Boyd, 2008; Cohen & Shade, 2008; Mazer, Murphy & Simonds, 2007; Papacharissi, 2009; Sawchuk & Shade, 2010; Stern & Taylor, 2007; Tong et al., 2008; Walther et al., 2008, 2009). Although much OSN research overlaps, the distinct areas of interest involve privacy issues (Boyd, 2008; Lenhart & Madden, 2008; Moscardelli & Divine, 2007; O'Neil, 2001; Tyma, 2007), risks and consequences of online behavior (Acar, 2008; Bradenburg, 2008; Mendoza, 2008); and online user behavior (Ellison et al., 2007; Hargittai, 2007; Livingstone, 2008; Shedlen, 2008).

Although computer-based communities date back to the early days of computer networks, it was only with the emergence of the commercial Internet that such communities became popular. Following the SixDegrees.com experience in 1997, hundreds of social networks were created online, which spurred the interest of academics in researching how individuals engage with online social networking sites and participate in various forms of online communities (Boyd, 2006; Boyd, & Ellison, 2007; Hinduja, & Patching, in press; Lenhart, & Madden, 2007; Livingston, 2004, p. 4; Stutzman, 2006).

Unlike the web, which is largely organized around content, OSN are organized around users and the content that they choose to share with others. Users join a network, create a profile, add content and establish links ("friendships") with other users, all of which often rely on the disclosure of personal information, that is, users' real names, details about age, location, personal photos and comments, for a wide audience of other users to see. The result is a social network that is utilized as a way for users to manage their identities, maintain social relationships among ever-widening circles of content, find users with similar interests and locate content and knowledge that has been contributed or endorsed by other users (Mislove et al., 2007). Potentially the most important benefit of online networks is probably, as Ellison, Steinfield and Lampe (2007) showed, the social capital resulting from creating and maintaining interpersonal relationships and friendships.

While the specific goals and patterns of usage among members of social networking sites may vary significantly across different services, they still tend to share a core of similar features such as a "profile." This is a representation of oneself for others to see with the intention of contacting or being contacted by others, to meet new friends or dates (Facebook, OkCupid, Match.com), find new jobs (LinkedIn), and share content (Flickr, Tumblr). Indeed the Social Software Weblog2 now groups hundreds of social networking sites into nine categories including business, common interests, dating, face-to-face facilitation, friends, pets and photos.

According to Gross and Acquisti (2005), while social networking sites tend to share similarities, three patterns of personal information revelation vary across different social networks: pretense of identification, type of information revealed, and visibility of information. First, with regard to identification issues, some sites (like Facebook) encourage the use of real names to (re)present an account profile to the rest of the online community (through technical specifications, registration requirements, or social norms), while other sites filter these names (in dating/connecting sites like Friendster) and some even openly discourage the use of real names (such as dating websites like Match.com). However, most sites do encourage the publication of personal and identifiable photos (such as clear shots of a person's face). Second, although the information usually revealed on such sites pertains to users' hobbies and interest, this is also often expanded to include information on users' current and previous schools and employers (as in Facebook); private information such as drinking and drug habits and sexual preferences and orientation (as in Match.com); and open-ended entries (as in LiveJournal). Third, the extent to which such information is made visible is highly variable. While some sites allow all members to view another member's profile, other sites (like Facebook) allow the user to control and limit the amount of information on their profile (i.e., photos, interests) that other members can view. Access to personal information may be limited to participants who are part of the direct or extended network of the profile owner (Gross & Acquisti, 2005).

Studies of the first popular social networking site, Friendster (Boyd, 2004, 2006, Boyd, & Heer, 2006, Donath, & Boyd, 2004) describe how members create their profiles with the intention of communicating news about themselves to others. Boyd, using an ethnographic approach, reveals the possibility of unintended consequences thus demonstrating that concerns raised by navigating issues of privacy and trust were apparent in the first scholarly articles on social networking sites. And yet, across different sites, anecdotal evidence suggests that participants are happy to disclose as much information as possible to as many people as possible. Therefore, while these networks facilitate interaction and communication among members, they also raise privacy and security concerns. Over the years social networks have evolved and adopted new features and technologies. For example, social networking platforms have extended their functionality beyond the confines of a website to mobile apps. Furthermore, many platforms provide an application-programming interface (API) that allows other technologies, such as other websites and mobile "apps," to use some of the features and data available in the website platform (Ellison, & Boyd, 2013). Third-party apps also enable users to share content across multiple social networking sites, as exemplified through platforms, such as Instagram, which enable users to post on Facebook and Twitter at the same time. Thus, the boundaries between social media platforms are less pronounced than they previously were (Ellison, & Boyd, 2013).

ONLINE NETWORKS AND SOCIAL NETWORK THEORY

A complex relationship exists between individuals' social network and their expectations of privacy. While individuals may be comfortable sharing personal information with a small group of friends, it might also follow that they are willing to share other types of personal information with a large circle of anonymous strangers.

One way to analyze how the involvement of individuals in social networks, in this case, OSN, helps to explain the behavior and attitudes of network members toward privacy concerns and disclosure (Garton, Haythornthwaite & Wellman, 1997) is by applying a social network analysis. A social network here refers to a "set of people (or organizations or other social entities) connected by a set of social relationships, such as friendship, co-working or information exchange" (Garton, Haythornthwaite & Wellman, 1997). This approach discusses the relevance of relations of different depth and strength in a person's social network and how such relationships influence the flow of information across different nodes within the network (Berkowitz, 1982; Gross & Acquisti, 2005; Wellman, 1988; Wasserman & Faust, 1994).

Strahilevitz applies social network analysis to privacy concerns, specifically as a tool to help interpret privacy in legal cases. According to Strahilevitz (2005), a person's expectations of how knowledge is expected to flow from node to node in a social network should influence that person's expectation of information privacy revealed in the network (Gross & Acquisti, 2005).

However, it is important to highlight the differences between offline and OSN. Firstly, OSN's are traditionally a forum for the younger generation, as according to market research, only 10% of online socializers are older than 55 years old, and close to 50% of online socializers are younger than 35 (Levin & Sanchez-Abril, 2009). Secondly, all interactions which occur on online social networking sites are recorded and retained, while offline, most social transactions leave no trace (Lessig, 1998). Finally, offline networks are made up of ties that can only be loosely categorized as weak or strong. In reality these ties are extremely diverse in terms of how close and intimate a subject perceives a relation to be, whereas OSN reduce relationships to binary relations, "friend or not." The term "friend," which is used to refer to all socializers, is virtually meaningless as many of a user's "friendships" are based on ties that are so weak that they would be nonexistent offline. Online networks, thus, are much larger than offline networks and have substantially more weaker ties. This may make OSN an "imagined" community. Therefore, trust in and within OSN are often assigned differently and have different meanings than when applied to offline social networks. Intimacy, while often associated with the disclosure of private information to certain individuals, now expands to include the disclosure of personal information to a large and potentially unknown number of friends and strangers altogether (Gross & Acquisti, 2005). The making of "friends" online for the sake of mere accumulation of a large number of "friends" as a status symbol is a growing online social phenomenon in itself (Giordano, 2006).

ONLINE NETWORKS AND PRIVACY

OSN constitute a new sphere for examining the loss of privacy, as not only are the participation rates in OSN staggering, with over one million self-descriptive personal profiles estimated to be available across different web-based social networks in the United States (Gross & Acquisti, 2005) among certain demographics; so, also, are the amount and type of information participants freely reveal (Schrammel et al., 2009; Venkat et al., 2014; Liu et al., 2011).

Participants voluntarily share their literary or entertainment interests, as well as political and sexual orientation. Furthermore, personal data (as well as contact information) is often provided, along with intimate photos documenting a person's social life (Gross & Acquisti, 2005).This occurs even though they are not required by the social network site itself. The fact that social network sites so deeply penetrate their users' everyday lives often leads to unintended consequences, such as threats to privacy and changes in the relationship between the public and private sphere. These issues have been studied with respect to a variety of Internet contexts and applications (Berkman & Shumway, 2003; Cocking & Matthews, 2000; Hamelink, 2000; Hinman, 2005; Iachello & Hong, 2007; Liu et al., 2011; McKenna, & Bargh, 2000; Pankoke-Babatz & Jeffrey, 2002; Spinello, 2005; Tavani & Grodzinsky, 2002; Venkat et al., 2014; Weinberger, 2005).

The very nature of social networks makes their security and network access controls weak, that is, registration, sharing and accessing data are made uncomplicated in order to leverage their value as network goods and to increase their overall appeal. Indeed, OSNs are usually for profit businesses and the computer servers on which the website is hosted, as well as any intellectual property related to the OSN, are usually the property of the OSN. Therefore, as profit-motivated businesses, OSNs have the fundamental objectives of attracting as many members as possible. This is combined with the fact that the cost of storing data continues to decline, thus implying that information provided on social networks is, in effect, public data that may exist for as long as anyone has an incentive to maintain it (Acquisti & Gross, 2006).

Although their network members do not pay dues, they have a loose contractual relationship with the OSN provider in the form of the OSN's terms of service. OSN providers act as the hub for all of their members' information and contacts (Levin & Sanchez-Abril, 2009). The creation and preservation of this social capital is systematically built upon the voluntary disclosure of private information to a virtually unlimited audience. As such, Ibrahim (2008) characterized online networks as "complicit risk communities where personal information becomes social capital which is traded and exchanged" (p. 251).

Several studies have found that users continually negotiate and manage the tension between perceived privacy risks and expected benefits (Ibrahim, 2008; Tufekci, 2008; Tyma, 2007). Social network site users are found to express higher risk-taking attitudes than individuals who are not members of an online network (Fogel & Nehmad, 2008).

When examining issues of online privacy, we must distinguish between collecting information, in itself a violation of privacy, and the publication and commercial use of this information, which constitutes an infringement and further violation of privacy. While the Internet-surfing public is generally aware of the possible dangers pertaining to disclosing personal information online (LaRose and Rifon, 2006, pp. 1009–1029), it is likely that this public does not make a connection between the seemingly insignificant pieces of information it spreads around the net and the ways in which this information may be used to violate their privacy in the future. For example, many users consent to receiving convenient and attractive services (free of charge) in exchange for disclosing various pieces of personal information, which can then be turned into an asset to be sold to advertisers.

The ease with which users interact and disclose personal information online can lead to risks of cyber-stalking and cyber-bullying. Other risks include significant financial losses (over 50 billion dollars in losses) as over 15 million US citizens fall victim to identity theft a year, damage to one's reputation, as was the case of a US teacher who was fired when inappropriate photos of her surfaced online (Fitzpatrick, 2008), and even violence. Such private information can also serve the interests of commercial companies as many corporations are striving to create "collective intelligence by combining information gathered on the Internet with DNA samples" (Lemelshtrich-Latar and Nordfors, 2009, pp. 10–24). These corporations are able to demonstrate our digital identity from genetic, psychological and sociological perspectives.

Such information is likely to be used, without any controls whatsoever, by commercial companies interested in behavioral focus.

For this reason, it is argued that even today one's privacy may be violated through one or more of the four different types of privacy exposure outlined above, by the inadvertent publication or disclosure of personal information. This is especially true with regard to social networks, and more specifically, Facebook, which is the most popular social network, as rumors or gossip deriving from social networks can harm an individual's reputation and good name. Social network users are already subject to harassment or monitoring which are enabled by various functions on these websites and are able to use the personal information of others or to transfer this information to third parties. In addition, computer hackers can steal identities or hack private accounts (Boyd, 2008, pp. 13–20; Boyd & Ellison, 2008, pp. 210–230). Thus, the reputations of social networking sites have been diminished by a number of incidents publicized by the news media (Chiaramonte & Martinez, 2006, Hass, 2006; Mintz, 2005; Read, 2006).

THE IMPORTANCE OF PRIVACY TO SOCIAL NETWORK USERS: CIRCLES OF PRIVACY

Is privacy really so important to Internet users? The right to privacy can be justified and explained in many ways, all related to individuals' ability and desire to control the information related to their personal lives and to protect themselves against intervention, penetration and exposure by others. Nevertheless, the right to privacy is based upon an individual's aspiration and desire to maintain circles of privacy. Circles of privacy refer to the new distinctions that are replacing the old and familiar distinction between the private, intimate and narrow sphere and the public and open spheres. The new circle is no longer private, personal and intimate, and is no longer relevant only to one's home, family or spouse. The new private sphere is much broader. It is a new circle of privacy that includes "friends," some of whom are near or complete strangers. This still is a circle of privacy, which many take the trouble to define and maintain. However, this circle no longer preserves classic American privacy, limited to the theory that "a man's home is his castle." Rather, it redefines the terms of privacy under the new technological reality.

This basic element of the right to privacy has been examined time and time again in the modern era, in view of the extreme ease with which many relinquish their privacy and agree to provide personal information and even to reveal their personal and private world to outside circles.

Until recently it was taken for granted that privacy was important to everyone and that every person wants to control the extent of the information known and published about him/herself. Privacy was perceived as an important aspect of individual dignity and the ability to maintain intimate relationships, as well as a tool for creating trust, community and even a functioning democracy (Solove, 2007, p. 745).

Traditional privacy research often suggests that individuals balance the choice between whether to disclose or keep certain information private. This choice involves the management of privacy boundaries and decisions about whom to include within those boundaries (Altman, 1975; Petronio, 2012). Recently, however, these assumptions have been questioned as Internet users demonstrate the exact opposite on a daily basis. Studies have indicated that users will express very strong concerns about privacy of their personal information, but will be less than vigilant about safeguarding it (Awad and Krishnan, 2006). In fact, Internet users disclose a great deal of personal information online. This disclosure not only occurs by sharing their personal preferences (the fourth category above), often inadvertently, but also directly by providing personal information, posting pictures and revealing elements of their identity.

FACEBOOK

Facebook is one of the most popular destinations on the Internet today (Arrington, 2010), dominating online communication and comprising over 900 million daily active users and 1.44 billion monthly active users as of March 31, 2015. Collectively, Facebook users disseminate more than 30 billion pieces of content per month to audiences chosen by their creators. (*Facebook News Room: Statistics*, http://newsroom.fb.com/company-info/ (last visited May 11, 2015). Facebook has transformed into a "simple, one-stop, all-purpose, habit-forming site for everyone from the underage to the golden-aged, neophytes to techies, gamers to political activists, and even pets to corporations" (Semitsu, 2011, p. 4).

While Facebook began as a social networking site for colleges and universities, it quickly expanded to encompass all types of users. The great popularity of the Facebook social network has motivated examination of the privacy awareness of its users (Acquisti & Gross, 2006; Bernhard et al., 2009, pp. 83–108; Lampe, Ellison & Steinfield, 2007; Stutzman, 2006). These researchers discovered that while Facebook users claimed to understand the issue of privacy, they still disclose a great deal of personal information. The explanation is that online users see privacy risks as something amorphous that is relevant to others but not to themselves. This finding coincides with the *third person effect*, which describes individuals' belief that media influences others much more than themselves. Those who reported feeling that their privacy had been invaded made sure to change their privacy settings on the website, whereas those users who had not experienced any invasion of privacy neglected to do so. Bernhard and colleagues (2009) also revealed that even though a relatively high number of Facebook users changed their privacy settings so that only friends could view their profile, it is difficult to define who a "friend" is (pp. 83–108). Many Facebook members approve friend requests from people they have only heard about from others, and some even approve all friend requests, regardless of previous acquaintance.

An additional motivation for managing Facebook privacy was found in a study by Lewis, Kaufman and Christakis (2008, pp. 79–100) examining the student-aged population in the United States. This study argued that online privacy habits are a result of both social influence and personal incentive. Students maintain a private profile (limited to friends) only if their friends have a similar privacy setting. With respect to gender, it was found that women tend to set a higher privacy level than men. Moreover, privacy habits are related to extent of use: users who are more active online are more aware of privacy issues and therefore set their privacy settings higher. In a similar study, Acquisti and Gross (2006, p. 17) found that even though students who use Facebook are aware, both generally and theoretically, of the risks of privacy violations, they are not aware of the extent to which the personal information they share on Facebook is exposed and visible. They claimed to trust the system, though in fact 77% of them had never even read Facebook's privacy policy (Acquisti & Gross, 2006, p. 17). Yet Facebook users are always one embarrassing photo away from their reputation being instantly ruined and ravaged before their entire network of family, friends, classmates, and colleagues. According to one study, 8% of companies with one thousand employees or more have terminated at least one employee for comments posted on a social networking site (Ostrow, 2009; Semitsu, 2011).

Facebook Places (O'Dell, 2010) is an example of a social network application that challenges perceptions of online privacy. It is one of a few new location-based applications (Dybwad, 2010) that enable Smartphone users to report their physical whereabouts as well as report their location to their friends and other Facebook members. It is a great tool for keeping in touch and for promoting business.

However, the new technology does not come without privacy concerns (Warren, 2010). Similar to the way a friend can tag another friend in a Facebook picture, friends can tag their friends into a location, whether or not they are actually there. Another issue is that third parties can monitor the location of the users of Facebook Places and outline their whereabouts and consumption patterns. This means that once third parties, including those with commercial or other interests have access to a Facebook Places location (or to Facebook accounts, depending on privacy settings), they can see users of Facebook Places even if they are not their Facebook friends. As argued below, this is a sacrifice users are (and perhaps even should be) willing to make in exchange for the sense of community and belonging that is derived from such exposure. All of the above create a new reality marked by a loss of privacy for those who use social networks.

Another privacy concern raised by OSN has to do with the collection of a large amount of personal user information. Data rich sites, such as social networks, then use this data to allow advertisers to target and personalize ads, thus receiving revenue through advertising. Currently, social networking websites account for one-third of all online display advertising (Marshall 2011). Sengupta and Rusli (2012) discussed the commercial use of users' personal data and observed that Facebook, the world's largest social network, was a fast churning data machine that captured and processed every click and interaction on its platform. As such, the network has repeatedly come under fire for using members' information for targeted ads. In 2014, Facebook let partnered advertisers leverage its members' data to deliver targeted ads to them on outside sites, particularly on mobile devices (Miners, 2014). The incident raised questions over the privacy implications for users, and whether this constitutes a new level of intrusion on people's data. The issue is controversial, because while some consumers may perceive personalized ad content more appealing and more aligned with their interests (Anand & Shachar, 2009; Lambrecht & Tucker, 2013), others may view it as an invasion and a violation of their privacy (Stone, 2010).

The concept of ads following you around the Internet is not new. People's browsing activity already factors into the ads they see on Facebook (as well as on Google and other sites) (Miners, 2014). However, the issue here is that Facebook data is being put to greater use for the purpose of targeting advertisements on sites far beyond Facebook. This raises, and will continue to raise many questions regarding privacy and privacy disclosure online.

But are Facebook users aware of these risks? Further research shows that despite privacy concerns, individuals disclose a great deal of personal information (Acquisti & Gross, 2007; Youn, 2005). For example, Bernhard Debatin et al. (2009) investigated Facebook users' awareness of privacy issues and perceived benefits and risks of utilizing the social network. They found that users claimed to understand privacy issues, yet reported uploading large amounts of personal information. Their research also found that individuals ascribed privacy risks more to others than to themselves, but were also more likely to change privacy settings when they were personally affected by privacy invasion than merely hearing about others' privacy invasions (Venkat et al., 2014).

Facebook's Privacy Policy

Over its short existence, Facebook has repeatedly changed its privacy policies. Sometimes the changes have been to the dismay of those concerned
about privacy. At other times, the changes were in response to uproars about
privacy. Facebook's policies initially shifted from a default assumption of
privacy to a default assumption of openness. Moreover, the policies have
tended to shift from complete control over all information to partial control
(Opsahl, 2010; Semitsu, 2011). However, in 2014, Facebook released a new
privacy policy, shortening its complex and legalese-loaded privacy policy by
two-thirds (from 9,000 words to just 2,700, and from multiple pages to just
one page), in hopes of making it more user-friendly (Lapowsky, 2014). The
policy change "introduced an easy-to-use privacy control interface, reduced
the amount of information that was automatically required to be displayed,
and also gave users new controls over how their personally identifiable data
could be tracked or used by third parties" (Tucker, 2014). The new interface,
the Privacy Basics Page, was launched as a hub for answers to the most popular questions asked on Facebook, such as how to un friend someone and block
users (Burnham, 2014). Facebook also accepted public comments from users
to help inform the policy.

Yet, while Facebook's privacy policy may now be easier to understand,
it doesn't make it easier for users to keep their information private on the
network. Facebook changed the default audience setting for new user posts
from "public" to "friends," and users can choose to opt-in or out of sharing
information with third-party apps. However, they still don't have the option
to select what type of information is shared (Lapowsky, 2014). Most importantly, the new data policy still maintains that Facebook has the right to use
information people share on Facebook to target ads to them on and off Facebook, without giving users the option to control what information is being
used for such advertising (Lapowsky, 2014).

Facebook introduced this improved privacy interface after being heavily
criticized for its complicated privacy settings. Bilton (2010) points out in
the national press that Facebook's privacy policy was longer than the United
States Constitution. Indeed, users who wanted to manage their Facebook
privacy settings had to go through about 50 categories, which then required
choosing among a total of more than 170 options, and monitoring the constant
changes Facebook makes in its privacy options and default settings. Publications like the *Washington Post* devoted entire pages to simply attempting to
help Facebook users set privacy options (Perez, 2008; Semitsu, 2011; Tucker,
2014).

Facebook had previously attracted negative publicity for trying to reduce
the amount of control users had over their data. This came to light in

December 2009 when ten privacy groups filed a complaint with the Federal Trade Commission over changes to Facebook's privacy policy that included default settings that made users' status updates available potentially to all Internet users. Previously, the system encouraged users to make information available only to their friends and people in the same networks. However, while the simplified transition page allows people to choose to keep their old settings, the FTC complaint argues that the system is less private than it was before (Schofield, 2009).

Facebook's 2011 policy changes had three major components. First, all privacy settings were aggregated into one simple control so users didn't have to deal with 170 granular options. Second, users no longer had to make all their "friends" and "connections" public. Third, it was now easier for users to click a single button in order to opt out of third-party applications accessing their personal information. Not only does Facebook collect user information, but it also disseminates this data to about five hundred thousand third-party application developers (Perez, 2008; Semitsu, 2011). In general, these changes were received favorably. Chris Conley (2010), the chairman of the American Civil Liberties Union, wrote that the changes "are significant improvements to Facebook's privacy" (par. 4).

However, this change in privacy settings did not change how the advertising ads on Facebook were targeted or whether advertisers could use user information to personalize ads. This means that though users were given control over how much information was being shared publicly and the extent to which they could be tracked by third parties, the actual mechanism by which the ads were targeted and served did not change.

Then, in 2014 Facebook initiated a new privacy policy (as outlined at the beginning of the chapter) which aimed to better clarify its privacy policy and protect users' privacy. As mentioned, the most significant change was that it changed the default audience for new members' posts from "public" to "friends," thus giving users more control over who sees their information.

Thus, Facebook's immense popularity challenges the traditional perception of privacy. Tens of millions of Internet users worldwide, and in Israel as well, have quickly, readily and without reservations adopted a tool which is changing their perception of privacy and their interactions with the world.

In their study on new media and in Israel, Lavie-Dinur and Karniel (2012) examined the use of social network sites with respect to privacy issues.

NEW MEDIA PRIVACY IN ISRAEL: A CASE STUDY

Israelis are among the world's heaviest Internet users as an estimated 74% of Israel's population use the Internet, compared to 77.3% in the United

States ("Internet Usage," 2015). Furthermore, Israelis have quickly and readily embraced the use of social networks, and, namely, the use of Facebook. In fact, as of August 2010, there were over 3 million Facebook users in Israel. Compared to the US, where only 60.4% of Internet users belong to Facebook, no less than 85.3% of Israeli Internet users are Facebook members. In Israel, as in the rest of the world, public and legal discourse has focused on confronting the challenges facing the right to privacy in new media.

The main privacy concerns related to the Internet, including the loss of privacy on social networks, are prevalent across the globe, as they are in Israel. Nevertheless, Rivka Ribak (2007) has attempted to analyze these issues in the context of Israeli journalists and the discussion of online privacy (Ribak & Lemish, 2007). Her analysis is divided into three arenas: the US, Israel and the global community of Internet users. Ribak (2007) claims that the discourse on online privacy stems from American concerns about the violation of norms that are common in the US. In other words, Ribak (2007) challenges the popular view that the demand for privacy is universal and proposes examining it in the local context.

Specifically, Ribak outlines the difference between the way privacy is viewed in the US and in Israel. She claims that in the US, privacy is viewed as a human right that is inevitably violated by advanced communication technologies, and thus needs to be protected, while in Israel the notion of privacy is more fluid, and is viewed as both a "crucial ingredient in any informed discussion about the Internet and as a foreign concept that is not rooted in or resonant with the local Israeli culture" (Ribak, 2007, p. 10). She attributes these differing perceptions of privacy to differences in privacy cultures, and the myths from which they originate. Therefore, while in the US the common myth is that of the lone individual "pioneer in the Wild West, suspicious of any central government, whereas in Israel it is of the pioneering Kibbutznik—a member in a collective that was founded on an ethos of material and emotional-sharing" (Ribak, 2007, p. 5).

Avraham and First (2003), in their study of Israeli newspaper advertisements, found that Israeli society has been undergoing a process of Americanization which began around the 1960s, with American symbols often replacing Israeli ones. It is argued that this ongoing Americanization of Israeli culture is a result of both technological advancements and globalization. Furthermore, it has led to a convergence between the two myths outlined above. While on the one hand, Israelis identify with the American values of individualism, liberty, and freedom, on the other, they continue to uphold the collective ethos of community sharing and belonging on which Israel was founded. This has translated, among other things, into an increasing willingness on the part of Israelis, to join and actively engage in online social networks and forums and to incur the loss of privacy as a consequence of such willingness.

In her study, Ribak (2007) describes the popular website "Hevre" (Friends) as an example of an Israeli social network that represents the openness of information and lack of anonymity in Israel, compared to the type of privacy attributed to global Internet users. Based upon the discussion in the Israeli *Captain Internet* newspaper column about "Hevre," which lacks any reference to the issue of privacy, as well as describing violation of privacy as an American obsession, Ribak (2007) claims that in Israel, the discussion of online privacy is purely theoretical, context based and subject to ongoing negotiations between global and local systems. Ribak (2007) reinforces her arguments with research from places other than the US, such as England and Israel, that does not discuss privacy or that views it differently than American discourse.

Ribak's (2007) main argument, which we support and reinforce, is that indeed some of the privacy discourse in Israel originates from the US, yet the reality and online behavior patterns of Israelis paint a completely different picture. In this paper, we identify and distinguish the gap between the legal normative discourse popular in Israel, which devotes much effort in defending and protecting privacy, and the actual online behavior of Israelis, which indicates that they place far less importance on the value of privacy and on protecting personal information.

Birnhack and Elkin-Koren (2009) continue Ribak's (2007) argument that the discussion of privacy is subject to negotiation and that it should be examined in a local context. In their research (Birnhack & Elkin-Koren, 2009, pp. 4–46), they begin with the assumption that Israel has rules and regulations (for example, those determining the permitted scope and transparency of surveillance and requiring publication of terms of use) that must be enforced in the context of online privacy. This study highlights the aforementioned gap between the standard value of trying to define and protect privacy and the common reality, practice and technology in Israel, which do not place such great importance on this value. Birnhack and Elkin-Koren (2009, p. 45) examined 1360 active Israeli websites for compliance with information privacy regulations between 2003 and 2006, focusing primarily on notice and consent. The findings of their research indicated that most of the Israeli websites do not provide their users with the adequate degree of privacy protection dictated by law. The websites frequently collect information about their surfers, and very few, if any, provide a form of notice that information is being collected. Popular or "sensitive" websites owned by large commercial corporations demonstrate much greater compliance with legal requirements of the law and had the lowest number of privacy violations compared to private or public websites.

A particularly interesting finding of this study was that public and governmental websites demonstrated a low level of compliance with the law and with protection of privacy. Birnhack and Elkin-Koren (2009, p. 46) concluded that information privacy regulations should not be issued according to one-size-fits-all solutions, but rather they should be adapted to diverse online activity patterns. This conclusion is related to the argument made by Nissenbaum (2010, p. 147) that the issue is not to protect privacy by denying access or granting the right to control one's own information. She claimed that Internet users are not so much concerned about limiting the flow of information, but that they seek guarantees that information is disseminated in a way that is appropriate and suitable to various contexts (Nissenbaum, 2010, pp. 147–149). This, then, is a matter of integrity.

Caspi and Gorsky (2006, pp. 54–59) describe the strategy of Israeli Internet users with respect to privacy issues. They claim that online deception and impersonation are, among other things, the very result of facing the issue of privacy. As part of their study, they conducted an online survey among Israeli Internet users about the issue of deception. The survey revealed that despite claims that deception is common, only a third of Internet users are not forthcoming in disclosing information about their sex, age, residence, marital status and employment. This withholding of information derives both from concerns about privacy and from the enjoyment of assuming another identity (Caspi & Gorsky, 2006, pp. 54–59).

Another explanation for this low level of online deception is related to a global transition (not necessarily Israeli, as Ribak (2007) argues) that began ten years ago. Instead of hiding behind anonymous nicknames, the tide is shifting toward sharing one's true identity with as many people as possible, which results in the emergence of social networks based on our true identity, our everyday activities and our circle of friends. Indeed, tying one's real name to one's online identity was one of the key differentiators that set Facebook apart from other online sites. This was seen by the network as a way to limit users' bad online behavior and increase users' responsibility by linking their online actions with their offline identities, and users quickly obliged. However, while users may use their real names, Papacharissi's study on personal web pages (2002) demonstrates that individuals continue to feel compelled to enrich self-presentation online and are "constantly executing a carefully controlled performance through which self presentation is achieved under optimal conditions" (Papacharissi, 2002, p. 644).

Even though, as in the Israeli case, not all users hide their identity, Bailey (1991, p. 66) claims that deception is related to power and that the weak use lies to protect themselves from the strong. Furthermore, Woo (2006, pp. 949–967) asks whether we are prepared to demand the "right to lie" to achieve the right to privacy and thus change our inherent moral beliefs and values.

The implied answer is that it is wrong to prejudice existing morals and that we should seek other ways to cope with privacy violations and to demand the right to confidentiality. This right to anonymity was also recently recognized by the Israeli Supreme Court.

ANONYMITY IN ISRAELI SUPREME COURT RULINGS

In a ruling in March 2010 (L.C.A 4447/07), the Israeli Supreme Court recognized the right to anonymity as part of the right to privacy (*Rami Mor v. Barak E.T.C*, 2010). This case discussed an Internet user's right to anonymity following a talkback he wrote and posted online which the plaintiff (Rami Mor) claimed to be libelous and slanderous.

Anonymous talkbacks in response to news releases and reports on leading websites and other forums are quite prevalent in Israel. The Supreme Court established that the right to anonymity is part of freedom of expression, following a similar ruling by the United States Supreme Court. The Israeli Supreme Court also explicitly addressed the fact that the right to anonymity is part of the right to privacy, as it enables an individual to refrain from exposing and disclosing personal information and also prevents his private life from being visible. Supreme Court Justice Rivlin ruled that in the absence of specific legislation on the matter, a judicial order cannot be used to reveal the identity of an anonymous speaker, and thus he returned the issue to the Israeli parliament, the Knesset.

Electronic Trade Bill, 5768–2008 did indeed include an arrangement to reveal the identity of an anonymous Internet surfer—anonymity is maintained apart from one exception: when "there is substantial concern" that the content of the information posted online is a civil wrong or a violation of intellectual property. The bill has yet to be approved (Birnhack, 2010, pp. 125–26).

Since the Supreme Court ruling mentioned above, the Israeli Parliament (Knesset) has not enacted new legislation to address the issue, so that a unique legal and normative situation exists in Israel whereby Internet users enjoy broad rights to anonymity that can only be prejudiced in the case of acts and publications that constitute criminal offenses. In such an event, enforcement authorities can use their authority to lift the curtain of anonymity and expose the suspect's identity.

The Communications Data Law, which passed as an amendment to the Criminal Procedure Law in 2007—also referred to as the "Big Brother Law"—enables law enforcement agencies to receive a variety of sensitive data from the telecom companies (The Communications Data Law of 2007). Investigative authorities may request information about suspects, including the identity of a subscriber, the lists of calls the suspect made, IP data and more by either filing a request for a court order or ordering telecom companies to disclose information if needed to prevent a crime in an emergency. This law has evoked public outcry with respect to the non constitutional violation of privacy enabled by the law ("New law," 2007).

Notwithstanding the aforesaid—particularly with respect to revealing the identity of suspects of criminal acts—the official legal status in Israel provides for a broad right of anonymity. Although Israel provides for the sweeping protection of the right to anonymity, there exists the desire of many Israelis to disclose their names, their pictures and even their personal history, as can be observed on websites such as "Hevre" and Facebook.

INTERNET AND SOCIAL NETWORK USE IN ISRAEL

Israelis are addicted to the Internet. They are among the world's heaviest Internet users. According to surfing data for May 2010 collected and published by the American Internet marketing research company comScore, Israel is ranked second among the developed countries in its scope of Internet usage. The Israeli Internet user spends on average 38.3 hours per month online, a figure 60% higher than the world average of 24 hours a month, and second only to Canada. The average American Internet user, for example, spends 36.3 hours online each month. In Britain the average is 32.3 hours per month, and in Sweden, 28.9 hours. Indeed, more Israeli Internet users visit the Facebook site than they do YNET, Walla or Microsoft websites ("Alexa's top sites in Israel"), and Facebook use far surpasses other prominent websites as well.

For example, the over 4 million Israeli Facebook members are willing to provide a great deal of personal information, some of it quite sensitive (Cohen, 2013). Many Internet users describe their every move on websites such as Twitter or on personal blogs. Furthermore, many provide information to commercial bodies, such as banks, cell phone companies, credit card companies and government offices, which collect masses of information, stored in electronic databases.

The November 2009 TNS Teleseker Internet Monitor (TIM) survey found that 68% of all Internet users maintained a personal profile on at least one social network, compared to 50% in the previous year. The survey was among a representative sample of 800 Jewish Israeli Internet users aged 13 and above. Similarly, teenagers and young adults report very high social network membership rates; 86% of Internet users aged 13–29 maintain a personal profile on at least one social network. The survey revealed that social networks are used primarily for communication purposes (37%), followed by status updates (29%), keeping in touch (24%) and looking at photos (16%), with games (15%) having the lowest rate of usage (Parag, 2010). Another finding of the survey is that 65% of Israeli Internet users believe that the level of transparency on websites is medium or low and that they are not clearly aware of which parts of their personal information are exposed to other Internet users and which are not.

In order to further investigate this, in 2011 we designed and administered a survey examining Internet use among 298 Israeli university students. The survey revealed that over 80% of participants spend the majority of their online time visiting social networking sites (with Facebook taking the lead at 88.9%). When asked about their online behaviors (relating to privacy), 44.4% of participants said they changed their privacy settings to allow only "friends" to view their profile, yet 74.6% of participants claimed to have never read Facebook's privacy settings. Almost half of the participants shared personal details (i.e., age, sex, birthday) and their photo with the general public—not just "friends." While nowhere close to a representative sample, the survey does reflect the gap between online behavior (sharing your personal details with the general public) and concerns over privacy (not even checking a site's privacy policy).

Facebook

Facebook is the most popular social network among Israeli Internet users. As of December 2013 there were 3,792,820 Facebook users in Israel ("Internet World Stats—Israel," 2015)—this number has nearly doubled since May 2012, when it stood at 2 million. Among them, 52% of Israeli Facebook users are men (1,671,660), and 48% women (1,433,060) (Cohen, 2013).

Furthermore, Facebook is ranked the third most visited website in Israel, according to Alexa rating ("Top Sites in Israel"). The rating orders sites by their 1 month Alexa traffic rank, which is calculated using a combination of average daily visitors and pageviews over the past month.

Twitter

Twitter does not publish official statistical data, but according to various Internet research companies it seems that Twitter has yet to become a major player among Israeli Internet users. The December 2009 TIM survey indicates that even though awareness of the Twitter Tweet service grew in the previous eight months from 18% to 69%, Twitter users constitute only 6.9% of Internet users. In August 2009, only 5% of Israeli Internet users used Twitter ("Most Israelis," 2010). In other words, in December 2009 around 300 thousand Israelis used Twitter, based upon 6.9% of 4.4 million Internet users.

Israeli Social Networks

The following data provide a more complete picture of the number of social network users in Israel. The data were obtained from Double Click and address the number of unique users of social networks in Israel as of May 2010. "Hevre": 47 thousand users; Mekusharim: 390 thousand users; The Marker Café: 430 thousand users; Beshutaf: 16 thousand; Twitter: 220 thousand; Facebook: 3.2 million. *Blog visitors:* IsraBlog: 180 thousand; Tapuz: forums and blogs together: 1.5 million; Reshimot: 93 thousand.

INTERNET USE PATTERNS AMONG ISRAELI YOUTH

A study of Internet use and purchases among young people over the age of 14 in Israel reveals some general online usage patterns (Rafaeli, Ariel & Katsman, 2009). Young people use the Internet mainly at home (99%), followed by at a friend's home (81%) and at school (46%). The frequency of use is high, with around three-quarters of the respondents reporting daily Internet usage. The preferred device used for surfing is a desktop computer (93%), although a third of the respondents reported using a laptop and another third mentioned their cell phone. The main uses cited for the Internet are watching video clips (80%), expanding general knowledge (79%) and downloading files (73%).

One of the most interesting differences between young people and adults is in the applications they use. Jones and Fox (2009) claim that adolescents view the Internet as a place for making personal contacts, whereas older people see the Internet as a tool for looking up information. In Israel this assumption is only partly confirmed. The three major online applications which most adults are using are e-mail, reading the news and looking up information to expand their general knowledge. For young people, on the other hand, the three most popular applications comprise watching video clips and expanding their general knowledge (80% and 79% respectively), followed by downloading files (including media files), reading the news and using instant messaging programs—73% for each application.

The most surprising finding is the major difference between young people and adults in their rate of instant messaging usage (Messenger, ICQ)—73% compared to 48%, respectively ($p < 0.01$). In addition, young people and adults differ significantly in e-mail usage (Ahonen, 2008). Teenagers use e-mail at lower rates than adults: 72% of the teenagers responded that they use e-mail on a regular basis, compared to 85% of the adults. This may be attributed to the growth of social networks in recent years and the greater presence of young people on these networks (Lipson, 2008). Possibly, youth may use social networks instead of instant messaging programs and e-mail.

CONCLUSION

Researchers worldwide have made various suggestions to handle violations of the right to privacy. Woo (2006, pp. 949–967) proposes that protecting the private sphere on the net requires focusing on the right to remain anonymous online or on the need to disguise one's identity to maintain confidentiality and ensure that privacy is not violated. This proposal represents a continuation of the usual and tolerable policy of maintaining confidentiality on the level of government and its various public bodies. According to Woo (2006, p. 949), this should now be applied in the personal-private sphere as well.

Lemi Baruh (2007, pp. 187–211) suggests that if there is no effective means to protect information about individuals surfing the Internet, they should at least be informed of the risks involved in each online activity. Baruh (2007) argues that risk categories should be created to describe how various institutions use data and exploit various user operations. This type of initiative reflects a demand that individuals be returned control over their identity and how it is represented and managed.

A survey concerned with people's trust in the Internet among 1200 adult Internet users in the US indicated that despite awareness of online risks, a considerable number of Internet users believe that commercial corporations or government institutions will help them protect their privacy and conceal information from other entities (Turrow and Hennessy, 2011, p. 3). This is to be accomplished through various laws that will outline clear rules about privacy, as well as a law that gives individuals the right to control the information collected about them by companies and a law that requires commercial corporations to finance courses on how to protect the privacy of Internet users.

Similar solutions have been proposed by various websites that understand and are attempting to respond to users' concerns about privacy violations. To this end, some websites offer privacy seals, powered by programs such as BBBOnLine seals and TRUSTe (LaRose & Rifone (2006, pp. 1009–1029). These websites are compared to other websites without such protection. In light of this, they found that websites that offered protection ironically required more personal information from surfers and in fact violated the privacy of online visitors more than websites that did not offer such protection. Therefore, the researchers claim that "naïve consumers who view seals as a form of privacy protection may be disappointed" (Larose & Rifone, 2006, pp. 1009–1029).

In addition, Lavie-Dinur and Karniel demonstrate that in Israel, as in the entire world, Internet users must contend with a new reality involving violations of privacy, collection of personal information about surfers, and commercial use of information for advertising and other purposes. Further, we believe that in Israel, more than elsewhere in the Western world, the approach to privacy is equivocal. On the one hand, public discourse has adopted privacy concepts from the United States, while on the other, Israeli culture is based on the history and values of Zionism, which center on relinquishing privacy in favor of other interests and values. We are thus witnessing a convergence between the American values of individualism and freedom, and the Israeli values of collectivism and community sharing and belonging.

In the past Israelis were willing to give up their individual privacy in the interest of society, the nation, the state, the army or the working population as a whole. Nowadays young Israelis are willing to give up their privacy with relative ease in favor of other interests and values, mainly for easy and convenient consumption of various media products, ease in surfing the Internet, and the desire for fame, self-promotion, information access and the ability to stay in constant contact with friends.

Israel is adopting social networks quickly and readily. Modeling itself on American law, Israeli law has placed great importance on the right to privacy and is even granting Internet users protection of their anonymity. Yet the reality in Israel and on social networks is different, with users readily waiving their privacy in favor of other interests and values.

REFERENCES

(2007). Approved by law—authority to monitor internet and cell phone users. *Ynet Online*. Retrieved from http://www.ynet.co.il/articles/0,7340,L-3483670,00.html.

(2010, January 13). TIM survey: most Israelis are members of social networks. Ynet Online. Retrieved from http://www.ynet.co.il/articles/0,7340,L-3833872,00.html.

Acquisti, A., & Gross, R. (2006). Imagined communities: awareness, information sharing, and privacy on the Facebook. In Danezi, G., & Golle, P. (Eds.,) *Proceedings of the 6th Workshop on Privacy Enhancing Technologies*, (pp. 36–58). Cambridge: Robinson College.

Ahonen, T. (2008). *Mobile as 7th of the Mass Media: Cellphone, cameraphone, iPhone, smartphone*. London: Futuretext.

Almog, O. (2000). *The Sabra: The creation of the new Jew*. Berkeley, CA: University of California Press, 226–33.

Altman I. (1975). *The environment and social behaviour*. Belmont, CA: Wadsworth.

Arrington, M. (2010, March 15). Hitwise says Facebook most popular U.S. site. *TechCrunch*. Retrieved from: http://techcrunch.com/2010/03/15/hitwise-saysfacebook-most-popular-u-s-site/.

Avraham, E., & First, A. (2003). "I buy American": The American image as reflected in Israeli Advertising. *Journal of Communication, 53*(2), 282–299.

Awad, N.F. & Krishnan, M.S. (2006). The Personalization privacy paradox: An empirical evaluation of information transparency and the willingness to be profiled online for personalization. *MIS Quarterly, 30*(1), 13–28.

Bailey, F.G. (1991). *The Prevalence of deceit*. Ithaca, NY: Cornell University Press, 66–125.

Baruh, L. (2007). Read at your own risk: shrinkage of privacy and interactive media. *New Media Society, 9*(2), 187–211.

Berkowitz, S.D. (1982). *An introduction to structural analysis: The network approach to social research*. Toronto: Butterworth.

Bilton, N. (2010, May 12). Price of Facebook privacy? Start clicking. *The New York Times*. Retrieved from http://www.nytimes.com/2010/05/13/technology/personaltech/13basics.htm 1?

Birnhack, M., & Elkin-Koren, N. (2009). Does law matter online? Empirical evidence on Privacy law compliance. *Social Science Research Network*, 5–46.

Birnhack, M. (2010, December 17). Unmasking anonymous users online. *Hukim Journal on Legislation, 2*, 125–126.

Boyd, D. (2008). Facebook's privacy trainwreck: Exposure, invasion and social convergence. Convergence: *The International Journal of Research into Media Technologies, 14*(1), 13–20.

Boyd, D., & Ellison, N.B. (2008). Social network sites: Definition, history and scholarship. *Journal of Computer-Mediated Communication, 13*, 210–230.

Brandtzaeg, P.B., Luders, M., & Sjetke, J.H. (2010). Too many Facebook 'friends'? Content sharing and sociability versus the need for privacy in social network sites. *Journal of Human Computer Interaction, 26*(11), 1006–1030.

Bronstein J. (2014). Creating possible selves: Information disclosure behaviour on social networks. *Information Research, 19*(1) paper 609. Retrieved from http://InformationR.net/ir/19-1/paper609.html

Buchanan, T., Paine, C., Joinson, A.N., & Reips, U. (2007). Development of measures of online privacy concern and protection for use on the internet. *Journal of the American Society for Information Science and Technology, 58*(2), 157–165.

Burnham, K. (2014). Facebook privacy policy updates: 4 facts. *Information Week*. Retrieved from http://www.informationweek.com/software/social/facebook-privacy-policy-updates-4-facts/d/d-id/1317481.

Cashmore, P. (2010, January 10). Facebook founder on privacy: Public is the new "social norm". *Mashable*. Retrieved from http://mashable.com/2010/01/10/facebook-founder-on-privacy/.

Caspi, A., & Gorsky, P. (2006). Online deception: Prevalence, motivation, and emotion. *Cyberpsychology and Behavior, 9*(1), 54–59.

Christofides, E., Muise, A., & Desmarais, S. (2009). Information disclosure and control on Facebook: Are they two sides of the same coin or two different process? *CyberPsychology & Behavior, 12*(3), 341–345.

Cohen, S. (2013, May 24). Facebook has 4 million Israeli users. *Ynet Online*. Retrieved from http://www.ynetnews.com/articles/0,7340,L-4383797,00.html

Conley, C. (2010, May 26). Facebook addresses several privacy problems. *Blog of Rights*. Retrieved from https://www.aclu.org/blog/content/facebook-addresses-several-privacy-problems].

Corbett, P. (2010). Facebook demographics and statistics report 2010–145% growth in one year, ISTRATEGYLABS (Jan. 4, 2010), Retrieved from: http://www.istrategy

labs.com/2010/01/facebook-demographics-andstatistics-report-2010-145-growth-in-1-year/.

Court of Justice of the European Union (2014). Fact sheet on the "Right to be Forgotten." Retrieved from http://ec.europa.eu/justice/newsroom/data-protection/news/140918_en.htm.

Criminal Procedure (Enforcement Powers—Communications Data) Law, pp. 5768 (2007). Retrieved from: http://www.loc.gov/law/help/online-privacy-law/israel.php.

Debatin, B., Lovejoy, J.P., Horn, A., & Hughes, B.N. (2009). Facebook and online privacy: Attitudes, behaviors, and unintended consequences. *Journal of Computer-Mediated Communication, 15*(1), 83–108. doi:10.1111/j.1083–6101.2009.01494.x

Decrew, J.W. (1997). *In pursuit of privacy: Law, ethics and the rise of technology.* Ithaca, NY: Cornell University Press, pp. 145–170.

Dickter, A. (2010, February 16). Google apologizes for Buzz fuss, stops automation. *Stanford Law School.* Retrieved from https://www.law.stanford.edu/news/google-apologizes-for-buzz-fuss-stops-automation.

Dybwad, B. (2010, January 23). Foursquare beats Yelp and Gowalla in reader poll. *Mashable.* Retrieved from http://mashable.com/2010/01/23/poll-foursquare-beats-yelp-and-gowalla.

Ellison, N.B., & Boyd, D. (2013). Sociality through social network sites. In W.H. Dutton (Ed.), *The Oxford handbook of internet studies,* (pp. 151–172). Oxford, UK: Oxford University Press.

Ellison, N.H., Heino, R., & Gibbs, J. (2006). Managing impressions online: Self-presentation processes in the online dating environment. *Journal of Computer-Mediated Communication, 11*(2), 415–441.

European Union Agency for Fundamental Rights. (2014). *Handbook on European data protection law.* Luxembourg: Publications Office.

Facebook Data Policy. (2015, January 30). Retrieved from https://www.facebook.com/policy.php.

Fitzpatrick, C. (2008). St. Lucie teacher: Bikini charter cost me my job. *The Palm Beach Post News.* Retrieved from http://www.palmbeachpost.com/treasurecoast/content/tcoast/epaper/2008/04/2 9/0429fishingteacher.html.

Fried, C. (1970). *An Anatomy of values: Problems and social choice.* Cambridge, MA: Harvard University Press.

Garton, L., Haythornthwaite, C., & Wellman, B. (1997). Studying online social Networks. *Journal of Computer-Mediated Communication, 3*(1), Retrieved from http://207.201.161.120/jcmc/vol3/issue1/garton.html.

Gibbs, S. (July 2, 2014). Facebook apologizes for psychological experiments on users. *The Guardian.* Retrieved from http://www.theguardian.com/technology/2014/jul/02/facebook-apologises-psychological-experiments-on-users.

Gross, R., & Acquisti, A. (2005). Information revelation and privacy in online social networks (the facebook case). Pre-proceedings *version*: *ACM Workshop on Privacy in the Electronic Society (WPES).*

Giordano, P. (2006). *How to get a lot of friends on MySpace,* EZINE ARTICLES, Retrieved from:http://ezinearticles.com/?How-To-Get-A-Lot-Of-Friends-On-MySpace&id=270277 (Apr. 9, 2009).

Internet usage, broadband and telecommunications reports. (2015, May 12). Retrieved from http://www.internetworldstats.com/me/il.htm.

Internet World States—Israel (2015, May 21). Retrieved from http://www.internetworldstats.com/middle.htm.

Jones, S., & Fox, S. (2009). *Generations online in 2009.* Washington, DC: Pew Internet & American Life Project, Pew Research Center.

Kane, G.C., Alavi, M., Labianca, G., & Borgatti, S.P. (2014). What's different about social media networks? A framework and research agenda. *MIS Quarterly, 38*(1), 275–304.

Karniel, Y., & Lavie-Dinur, A. (2012). Privacy in new media in Israel—How social networks are helping to shape the perception of privacy in Israeli society. *Journal of Information, Communication & Ethics in Society, 10*(4), 288–304.

Kleinman, A. (2014, May 22). Facebook just made a big change to privacy settings. *Huffington Post.* Retrieved from http://www.huffingtonpost.com/2014/05/22/facebook-privacy-settings_n_5372109.html.

Krishnamurthy, B., & Wills, C. E. (2008). Characterizing privacy in online social networks. *WOSN '08 Proceedings of the First Workshop on Online Social networks,* New York, NY.

Lambrecht, A., & Tucker, C. (2013). When does retargeting work? Information specificity in online advertising. *Journal of Marketing Research, 50,* 561–76.

Lapowsky, I. (2014, November 13). Facebook rolls out clearer privacy policy but you still can't control your data. *Wired Magazine.* Retrieved from http://www.wired.com/2014/11/facebook-revamps-privacy-policy/.

Larose, R., & Rifon, N. (2006). Your privacy is assured—of being disturbed: Websites with and without privacy seals. *New Media Society, 8*(6), 1009–1029.

Lavie-Dinur, A. & Karniel, Y. (2010). "Privacy and fame: Privacy cession and exposure techniques in Israel's Big Brother reality program." Unpublished manuscript.

Lemelshtrich-Latar, N., & Nordfors, D. (2009). Digital identities and journalism content. *Innovation Journalism, 6*(7), 10–24.

Levin, A., & Abril, P. (2009). Two notions of privacy online. *Vanderbilt Journal of Entertainment & Technology Law, 11*(4), 1001–1051.

Lewis, K., Kaufman, J., & Christakis, N. (2008). The taste for privacy: An analysis of college student privacy settings in an online social network. *Journal of Computer-Mediated Communication, 14,* 79–100.

Lilian, N. (2010, June 28). Not only eavesdropping: Trigger happy on communications Data. *Ynet Online.* Retrieved from http://www.ynet.co.il/articles/0,7340,L-3912050,00.html.

Lipson, N. (2008). All Israelis are friends—On social networks. *Captain Internet.* Retrieved from http://www.haaretz.co.il/captain/spages/1009248.html.

Liu, Y., Gummadi, K.P., Krishnamurthy, B., & Mislove, A. (2011). Analyzing Facebook privacy settings: User expectations vs. reality. Proceedings from the *SIGCOMM 2011 Conference, ACM* (2011), 61–70.

Livingstone, S. (2008). Taking risky opportunities in youthful content creation: Teenagers' use of social networking sites for intimacy, privacy and self-expression. *New Media & Society, 10*(3), 393–411.

Marshall, J. (2011, May 10). Facebook served a third of display impressions in Q 1. *ClickZ*, Retrieved from http://www.clickz.com/clickz/news/2069381/facebook-serveddisplay-impressions-q1.

Martin, K. (2012). Diminished or just different? A factorial vignette study of privacy as a social Contract. *Journal of Business Ethics, 11*(4), 519–539.

Miners, Z. (2014). Facebook privacy questions resurface. *PC World, 32*(12), 23–26.

Mislove, A., Marcon, M., Gummadi, K.P., Druschel, P., & Bhattacharjee, B. (2007). Measurement and analysis of online social networks. IMC '07 Proceedings of the *7th ACM SIGCOMM Conference on Internet Measurement*, New York, NY.

Most Israelis are members of social networks. (2010). *Ynet Online*. Retrieved from http://www.ynet.co.il/articles/0,7340,L-3833872,00.html.

New law regulates access to communications data (2007. December 18). Retrieved from http://it-law.co.il/news/israeli_internet_law_update/2007/12/18/new_law_regulates_ access_to_communication_data/?year=2010&month=4.

Nissenbaum, H. (2010). *Privacy in context: Technology, policy and the integrity of social life*, (pp. 120–149). Stanford, CA: Stanford University Press.

Nosko, A.W., Wood, E., & Molema, S. (2010). All about me: Disclosure in online social networking profiles. The case of Facebook. *Computers in Human Behavior, 26*(3), 406–418.

O'Dell, J. (2010, August 19). A field guide to using Facebook Places. *Mashable*. Retrieved from http://mashable.com/2010/08/19/facebook-places-guide.

Onn, Y. (2005). Privacy in the digital environment. In N. Elkin-Koren, N., & M. Birnhack (Eds), *Privacy in the digital environment* (pp. 2–167). Haifa, Israel: Haifa Center of Law and Technology.

Opsahl, K. *Facebook's eroding privacy policy: A timeline*, EFF DEEPLINKS BLOG (2010, April 28), Retrieved from: http://www.eff.org/deeplinks/2010/04/facebook-timeline.

Oremus, W. (2014). Facebook's privacy pivot. *Slate Magazine*. Retrieved from http://www.slate.com/articles/technology/future_tense/2014/07/facebook_s_privacy_pivot_mark_zuckerberg_s_plan_to_win_back_trust.single.html.

Ostrow, A. (2009). Facebook fired: 8% of US companies have sacked social media miscreants, Mashable.COM (2009, August 10), Retrieved from: http://mashable.com/2009/08/10/social-media-misuse (discussing survey by Internet security firm Proofpoint).

Papacharissi, Z. (2002). The presentation of self in virtual life: Characteristics of personal home pages. *Journalism & Mass Communication Quarterly, 79*(3), 643–660.

Parag, N. (2010, March 10). "TIM February: Globes leads financial websites in surfing from work," Globes. Retrieved from http://www.globes.co.il/news/article.aspx?did=1000545594&fid=594.

Perez, S. (2010). *How to delete Facebook applications (and Why You Should)*, READ-WRITEWEB.COM, Retrieved from: http://www.readwriteweb.com/archives/how_to_delete_facebook_applications_ and_why_you_should.php (last visited November. 1, 2010).

Petronio S. (2002). *Boundaries of privacy: Dialectics of disclosure*. Albany: University of New York.

Preston, A. (August 3, 2014). The death of privacy. *The Guardian*. Retrieved from http://www.theguardian.com/world/2014/aug/03/internet-death-privacy-google-facebook-alex-preston.

Rafaeli, S., Ariel, Y., & Katsman, M. (2009). *Online youth: Internet use and shopping patterns*. Jerusalem, Israel: Research and Economic Administration, Ministry of Industry, Trade and Labor.

Rami Mor v. Barak E.T.C the Company for Bezeq International Services Ltd., L.C.A. 4447/07 (2010).

Ribak, R., & Lemish, D. (2007). "Israeli children go on-line," (article presented at the 11th Annual conference of the Israel Internet Association, Avenue Convention Center, Airport City, Lod, Israel, February 2007).

Schechner, S. (2015, April 2). Facebook privacy controls face scrutiny in Europe. *The Wall Street Journal*. Retrieved from http://www.wsj.com/articles/facebook-confronts-european-probes-1427975994.

Schofield, J. (2009, December 17). Privacy groups file FTC complaint against Facebook. *The Guardian*. Retrieved from http://www.theguardian.com/technology/blog/2009/dec/17/facebook-privacy-ftc-complaint.

Schrammel, J., Kiffel, C., & Tscheligi, M. (2009). How much do you tell?: Information disclosure behaviour indifferent types of online communities. In Carrol, J.M. (ed.) *Proceedings of the Fourth International Conference on Communities and Technologies*, (pp., 275–284). New York: ACM Press.

Semitsu, J.P. (2011). From facebook to mug shot: How the dearth of social networking privacy rights revolutionized online government surveillance. *Pace Law Review*, *31*(1), 291–381.

Sengupta, S., & Rusli, E.M. (2012, January 31). Personal data's value? Facebook is set to find out. *The NewYork Times*. Retrieved from http://www.nytimes.com/2012/02/01/technology/riding-personal-data-facebook-is-going-public.html.

Solove, D. (2007). I've got nothing to hide and other misunderstandings of privacy. *San Diego Law Review*, *44*, 745.

Stone, B. (2010, March 3). Ads posted on facebook strike some as OffKey. *The New York Times*. Retrieved from http://www.nytimes.com/2010/03/04/technology/04facebook.html?_r=0].

Strahilevitz, L.J. (2004). A social networks theory of privacy. The Law School, University of Chicago, John M. Olin Law & Economics Working Paper No. 230 (2D Series).

Stutzman, F. (2006). An evaluation of identity-sharing behavior in social network communities. *Proceedings of the 2006 iDMAa and IMS Code Conference*, Oxford, Ohio. Top sites in Israel. Retrieved from http://www.alexa.com/topsites/countries/IL.

Travis, A., & Arthur, C. (2014, May 13). EU court backs 'right to be forgotten': Google must amend results on request. *The Guardian*. Retrieved from http://www.theguardian.com/technology/2014/may/13/right-to-be-forgotten-eu-court-google-search-results

Tucker, C.E. (2014). Social networks, personalized advertising, and privacy controls. *Journal of Marketing Research (JMR)*, *51*(5), 546–562. doi:10.1509/jmr.10.0355.

Turow, J., & Hennessy, M. (2011). Internet privacy and institutional trust: Insights from a National Survey. *New Media and Society*, *9*, 300–318.

Urieli, N. (1989). "The cultural aspect of cigarette advertisements in Israel," (Thesis toward receipt of masters of social sciences, Tel Aviv University).

Venkat, A., Pichandy, C., Barclay, F.P., & Jayaseelan, R. (2014). Facebook privacy management: An empirical study of awareness, perception and fears. *Global Media Journal: Indian Edition*, *5*(1), 1–20.

Warren, C. (2010, August 19). Privacy group voices concern about Facebook places. *Mashable*. Retrieved from http://mashable.com/2010/08/18/aclu-privacy-facebook- places.

Wasserman, S., & Faust, K. (1994). *Social network analysis: Methods and applications*. Cambridge: Cambridge University Press.

Wellman, B. (1988). Structural analysis: From method and metaphor to theory and Substance. In Wellman, B. & Berkowitz, S.D. (Eds.), *Social structures: A network approach* (pp. 19–61). Cambridge: Cambridge University Press.

Woo, J. (2006). The right not to be identified: Privacy and anonymity in the interactive media Environment. *New Media Society*, *8*, 949–967.

Youn S. (2005). Teenagers' perceptions of online privacy and coping behaviors: A risk-benefit appraisal approach. *Journal of Broadcasting & Electronic Media*, *49*, 86–110.

Zimmer, M. (2014, February 4). Mark Zuckerberg's theory of privacy. *The Washington Post*. Retrieved from http://www.washingtonpost.com/lifestyle/style/mark-zuckerbergs-theory-of-privacy/2014/02/03/2c1d780a-8cea-11e3–95dd-36ff657a4dae_story.html.

Zweir, S., Araujo, T., Boukes, M., & Willemsen, L. (2011). Boundaries to the articulation of possible selves through social networks: The case of Facebook profilers' social connectedness. *CyberPsychology, Behavior, and Social Networking*, *14*(10), 571–576.

Chapter 5

Blogs

To be Popular . . . I'll Write it All Down

This chapter focuses on an analysis of privacy in the blogosphere, specifically with reference to blogs written by adolescent girls. Data shows that teenage girls who use virtual blogs in place of traditional diaries constitute the majority of bloggers. One feature of adolescence is adolescents' need to develop their own personality and identity and differentiate themselves from their family and friends. A diary is one of the means that adolescents use to express their true emotions and authentic desires, and their attitudes toward the events they experience and the people they encounter. Using a blog—a more private journal-like format—strongly reinforces the obliteration of boundaries between the public and the private.

An elementary ingredient of online media among youth around the world is indeed disclosing one's information, whether it is through Facebook posts, personal diaries, photos, friendships, content preferences and/or tracked locations, among others (Mayer-Schönberger, 2011). According to Boyd (2014), teenagers are searching for networks and communities of their own to give meaning to their lives. Social media have enabled them to create and participate in what she terms "network publics." These media play an enormous role in the lives of teenagers. Different social networks, video-sharing sites and micro blogging platforms, among other related tools, allow participants to create and share their personal content. However, she additionally quotes a 17-year-old teen who spends hours a day on social networks, and who states: "Just because teenagers use internet sites doesn't mean they don't care about privacy" (Boyd, pp. 54–77). In addition, teenagers, more often than not, harbor a sense of entitlement to their "right to privacy." Yet this desire for privacy, in appearance, seems to contradict the growing popularity of teenage blogs, where blog users (teenagers and others) regularly expose their private selves in the public sphere. A revealing example of the salience of the contradiction between a desire for privacy and actual exposure through blogging can be found in this example of a teenager's plea for her mother to stay out of her blog. The teenager writes, "By the way, mom, if you're reading this . . . do not come here again . . . ever . . . I don't understand, what is your problem?? First you go through my diary and then my blog??" (Vaisman, 2011).

This chapter explores the changing nature and perception of privacy through an analysis of teenage girls' online blogs. Our study seeks to examine what kind of information teenage girls reveal in their blogs as well as the level of privacy exposure they engage in.

WEBLOGS

Today, blogs or weblogs constitute one of the most widely embraced and easy-to-use "Internet publishing tools" (Richardson, 2009, p. 2) and are used extensively in the popular media as well as in political campaigns, news organizations, businesses and classrooms. Blogs are websites containing dated entries in reverse chronological order, so that the most recent entry appears first, and as they are participatory, they allow for comment and dialogue among author and readers (Benson & Favini, 2006; Gunter, 2009; Lee & Bates, 2007). A fundamental difference between blogs and other web-based publishing sites, such as personalized home pages is that rather than substituting new materials for old, a blogger continuously adds new posts, creating a growing compilation of entries and an archive of previous posts (McCullagh, 2008). Blogging has gained popularity over the past decade as part of a bigger trend toward micro publishing: increased publishing and distribution tools on the Internet, accessible to all (Vaisman, 2011).

In the early days, blogs were primarily web pages containing links to other useful resources and were usually maintained manually (Blood 2004). According to some, the earliest blog was created by Tim Berners-Lee in 1991 (Winer, 1999). However, what is commonly recognized as the present-day format first appeared in 1996, and the term weblog was first coined in 1997 (Blood, 2004; Herring, Scheidt, Bonus & Wright, 2005). In late 1999, free blog software and blog hosting sites became widely available and the number of blogs grew significantly (Blood, 2000). According to Blogpulse. com, a site that tracks blogging trends, in 2010 there were 126,861,574 blogs in existence, 42,234 blogs created every 24 hours, and 889,254 blog posts occurring every hour ("Blogpulse Stats," 2010; Sanderson & Kassing, 2011). Moreover, according to the Technorati (social media ad network) 2013 Digital Influence Report, blogs rank among the top five "most trustworthy" sources, when compared to other sources for information on the Internet.

There are a number of weblog genres including news and celebrity blogs as well as educational and professional ones where bloggers can write about almost anything: personal stories, fashion, food, ideas, reviews, opinions, feelings and more. Bloggers interact with one another in different manners, such as by subscribing to another blogger, commenting on a blog entry (post), or citing the content of a blog entry. These activities build the interactive relations between bloggers and their readers (Lin & Kao, 2010) and form a complex social network, which is often called the blogosphere (Chau & Xu, 2012). Thus, through the interaction and communication between bloggers, information, ideas, propaganda, and opinions spread throughout the blogosphere (Adar & Adamic 2005; Ali-Hasan & Adamic, 2007; Gruhl et al. 2004; Kumar et al. 2005; Nahon et al. 2011). Blogs vary depending on their context and are categorized in numerous ways, such as by technical and structural features, purpose, function, topic, authors, format, content and other defining characteristics (Aharony 2009; Kuhn 2007; Lee & Bates, 2007). Blog posts are mainly textual but may also include many different types of media (e.g., text, images, videos and voice recordings) through which a personality can more comprehensively be crafted and communicated (Sinanan, Graham & Jie, 2014). Such compilations of postings create a context for blog readers. Regular readers can get a sense of the identifying "voice" or "persona" behind the posts and over time, a blog archive can read like an evolving story of the blogger's interests and experiences.

One important reason why blogs are so prevalent is their ease of use; indeed, there is no new technology associated with blogs; rather, they are a reconfiguration of existing web-based tools and the wide variety of software applications and hosting sites available to users (Stefanone & Chyng-Yang, 2007). These tools allow anyone with access to a computer and the Internet to create and maintain a blog since so little technical knowledge (e.g., HTML) is required.

While many individuals use blogs to provide political commentary, most Americans use their blogs to record and reflect on their daily experiences (Lenhart & Fox, 2006) and these blogs typically take the form of online diaries, where private and intimate content is posted in daily, monthly and yearly snippets (Herring et al., 2004). People use personal blogs to record their daily lives and express their opinions and emotions (Gill et al., 2009; Nardi et al. 2004). The online diary is generally focused on the "drama" (Goffman, 1959) of everyday interactions, selves and situations. The narrative structure produced is linear, rigorously defined by chronology and has no sense of an ending.

Studies show that bloggers "engage in selective self-presentation strategies on their blogs," which are tailored to anticipated interaction with strangers, friends, or both (Becker & Stamp, 2005; Qian & Scott, 2007;

Tice, Butler, Muraven, & Stillwell, 1995). Personal journal blogs are more likely to be characterized by self-disclosure than filter blogs, which are devoted to external content like political news (Herring & Paolillo, 2006). Research suggests that blogs are often used to cultivate relationships (Hollenbaugh, 2011; Stefanone & Jang, 2007). Bloggers maintain various levels of anonymity on their blogs (Qian & Scott, 2007; Westerman, Heide, Klein, & Walther 2008) as well as oftentimes constructing versions of reality for their lives and personal relationships (through both text and image) that may differ from lived experiences (Trammell & Keshelashvili, 2005; Vasalou & Joinson, 2009).

Frye and Dornisch (2010) found that Internet users considered public blogs to be the least private medium when compared to other forms of Internet communication. Blogging tools and hosting sites provide different levels of privacy, ranging from password-protected sites to publicly listed and accessible sites, although studies show that the overwhelming majority of users do not restrict access to content (Lenhart & Fox, 2006). Bloggers will often manage their degree of disclosure and anonymity by controlling the amount of identifying information they disclose on their blogs (Viegas, 2005), such as a person's name, age, location, schools attended, which an employer could consider as identity management cues.

Thus, by their very nature, blogs raise a number of privacy issues. On the one hand, they are persistent and cumulative. On the other hand, they are easy to produce and disseminate which results in large amounts of sometimes personal information being broadcast across the Internet (McCullagh, 2008). When compared to social network sites such as Facebook, blogs provide a more isolated space with less interactivity that may reduce users' awareness of their audiences. Thus, blog posts may be more revealing than those on social network sites.

Personal Blogs

Research has found that the majority of blogs maintained on the web are personal journal blogs (Herring, Scheidt, Wright, & Bonus, 2005; Viegas, 2005). These blogs feature content analogous to a personal diary or journal, composed of short posts concerning the blogger's life and internal self (Blood, 2002; Herring, Scheidt, Bonus, & Wright, 2004, 2005; Lenhart & Fox, 2006; Nardi, Gumbrecht, & Swartz, 2004). The literature refers to personal weblog writing as a "private" space even though it is available for the author's "public" consumption (Cadle 2005; Ratliff 2006). Indeed, studies examining the content of personal blogs reveal that personal experiences and private information make up the majority of blog content (Lenhart, & Fox, 2006; Qian, & Scott, 2007; Viegas, 2005).

For example, in a study by Viegas (2005), one-fourth of the respondents reported they posted very personal information on their blogs fairly often, whereas less than 20% claimed they never posted intimate information on their blogs. Herring et al. (2004, 2005) examined a random sample of blogs and found that more than 70% were personal journals, in which users generally posted regarding their day-to-day lives, often focusing on personal thoughts and feelings.

Higher amounts of disclosure in personal journal blogs are likely due to bloggers' motivations for maintaining these blogs. People are motivated to maintain personal journal blogs to archive and organize their thoughts, to help others, for social connection, to get feedback (Hollenbaugh, 2011), to express creativity and to entertain others (Lenhart & Fox, 2006). Indeed, Paechter (2013) argues that blogs allow individuals to take "backstage" events and bring them into the spaces of frontstage performance (p. 14), an example of putting the self "on view" (Graham, Rouncefield, & Satchell 2009, p. 268).

Karen McCullagh (2008) explored bloggers' subjective sense of privacy by examining their blogging practices and their expectations of privacy when publishing online. Her findings suggest that blogging offers individuals a unique opportunity to work on their self-identity via the degree of self-expression and social interaction that is available in this medium. This finding helps to explain why bloggers consciously bring the "private" to the public realm, despite the inherent privacy risks they face in doing so (McCullagh, 2008).

Research has shown that age impacts blogging behaviors and content. Specifically, younger people are more likely to blog about personal experiences while older bloggers are more likely to be motivated to blog to share their skills or knowledge with their readers (Lenhart, 2006). Indeed, 87 of 207 bloggers surveyed expressed concern about the potential ramifications of self-disclosure in their blogs (Qian & Scott, 2007). However, of those bloggers who were concerned, only 42% actually self-censored themselves when posting content in their blog entries. Although the concern for privacy seems to be there, bloggers do not appear to be taking actions to protect their private self-disclosures (Hollenbaugh & Everett, 2013; Qian & Scott, 2007).

There may also be a gender/age aspect to disclosing personal information on blogs. Although there is no significant difference between men and women in disclosing identifying information (Huffaker & Calvert, 2005), teenage girls do seem to disclose more intimate information in their blogs than teenage boys (Bortree, 2005). Additionally, Lenhart and Fox (2006) found that females were more likely than males to be inspired to post a personal experience on their blogs, which may suggest that they would disclose more in these posts.

Teenage Blogs

Many studies show that the Internet is popular among teenagers (Anderson, 2000; Calvert, Jordan, & Cocking, 2002; Lenhart, Madden, & Hitlin, 2005; Lenhart, Rainie, & Lewis, 2001; Livingstone & Bober, 2005; Rainie & Hitlin, 2005; Rainie & Horrigan, 2005; Rideout, Roberts, & Foehr, 2005). Moreover, Internet access has increased in classrooms (Livingstone & Bober, 2005; Parsad & Jones, 2005; Rainie & Hitlin, 2005), as well as in households (Livingstone & Bober, 2005; Rainie & Horrigan, 2005), where adolescents average at least one hour in front of a computer per day (Rideout et al., 2005). Furthermore, participation in virtual communities and social network sites is now firmly embedded in the culture of many young people who are growing up as digital natives (Palfrey & Glasser, 2008). These mediated interactions are reshaping processes of self-expression, identity-building and sociality.

Many teenagers are opting to use blogs to write about their experiences and instantly publish their thoughts and feelings to the web. Studies suggest that almost half of all blogs are created by teenagers (Huffaker & Calvert, 2005): 54% of bloggers are under the age of 30 (Lenhart & Fox, 2006). These blogs seem to provide teenagers with "an outlet for personal expression and reflection, as well as a way to communicate and connect with others" (Huffaker, 2006, p. 1). From a developmental perspective, blogs provide a platform where teens can present and explore their identity or identities online, an important aspect of identity exploration (Nurmi, 2004). Blogs, which are time-stamped, are thus conducive to telling stories or constructing narratives. They provide teens with a way to connect the events in their lives and even reflect upon them. From a social perspective, blogs can help teens create or maintain social ties. There are many components to blogging, such as commenting, links, and others, that can enhance social connections for teens, helping them to meet new people and maintain existing friendships online, which already accounts for much of teen use of the Internet (Lenhart et al., 2005; Rideout et al., 2005).

Teenage Girl Blogs

Adolescent girls have emerged as the largest demographic of bloggers in the United States (Davis, 2010). Indeed, most scholars agree that there seems to be the same affinity between women and diaries as between women and weblogs (Gilbert 1995; Haas et al. 2002; Herring, 2000, 2001; Herring et al., 2005; Takayoshy 2000). In particular, there is evidence to argue that "adolescent girls find personal weblogs to be a comfortable rather than a threatening space" (Cadle, 2005, p. 17). In fact, a recent study (Herring et al., 2005) found that while each gender accounts for about half of all weblogs, personal blogs are dominated by females of teen age and preferred by females in general (Nowson & Oberlander, 2006).

Boyd (2014), although not directly focused on girls alone, outlines the views and desires of thousands of teens, which she studied. She found that they do care about their privacy. However, the way that they understand privacy practices may not appear logical to adults. This resonates the basic argument that this book, *Privacy and Fame: How We Expose Ourselves Across Media Platforms*, aims to put forward, that people today, especially teens, are changing their concept of privacy as their technological opportunities for self-exposure or convenience are dramatically changing. Teens are generally less concerned with organizations and corporations, but rather sensitive to people who are paternalistic toward their behavior and monitor their lives, such as parents and teachers. Teenagers' desire for privacy does not undermine their eagerness to participate in public. Furthermore, Boyd's (2014) study confirms that teenagers do have a sense of privacy. However, teens internalize that other than adapting to the changing conditions, there is little that they can do to protect their privacy. They therefore adopt different practices and develop innovative solutions in order to achieve privacy in network publics. For example, they frequently change social platforms to avoid snooping parents. This is an expression of the way that teenagers perceive privacy in the digital age—they establish their own sense of privacy, as they are "aware" of the blurry boundaries between the private and public spheres.

Other studies (Lövheim, 2011; Harris, 2008; Chittenden, 2010) examine girls' and women's blogs within the context of uses of public spaces and the nature of public expression. For example, Lövheim (2011) demonstrates how young Swedish women's blogs negotiate individualized and commercialized ideals of femininity, such as autonomy, self-development and career, and normalized ideals of femininity, such as moderation, care and empathy. Chittenden (2010) suggests that how teenage girls "conceptualize their online visual representation may offer a resource for how they come to realize their offline identity" (p. 505). Furthermore, Harris (2008) argues that young women "write themselves into being" online, because they have little access to public expression and thus online participation is based on a desire to engage publically (p. 489).

Furthermore, the peer-to-peer community forming between bloggers resonates with the teenagers' need for reinforcements from their equals (Brown 2004a, Damon 1983). Bortree's (2005) study revealed that teenage girls disclosed very personal information about their despairs and frustrations, as well as other feelings. These respondents said they would not openly disclose these things face to face (Bortree, 2005).

However, it is important to note that while there are several benefits of blog use among teenagers, for both psychological and social development, studies also suggest some possible negative attributes of blog use (Huffaker, 2006). For example, the amount of personal disclosure on these blogs, especially real names, age and offline location, also makes teen bloggers susceptible to dangers such as cyber-stalking and sexual predation.

INFORMATION REVEALED: PRIVACY AND TEEN BLOGS

David Huffaker (2006) analyzed the content and characteristics of a random sample of teenage blogs in order to examine the extent to which teen bloggers present their identity online. His analysis found that the teenage bloggers reveal a considerable amount of personal detail online. Indeed, researchers have found that adolescents and emerging adults typically express themselves online in a manner that is consistent with their offline identity (Boyd, 2008; Gross, 2004; Huffaker & Calvert, 2005; Stern, 2007)—they tend not to create a fictitious or "pretend" identity in their online writings, but rather disclose personal information such as real name, age and location in the offline world. For example, Huffaker (2006) found that personal information most often disclosed includes first name (70%), age (67%) and contact information (61%) in the form of e-mail (44%), instant messenger name (44%) or a link to a personal home page (30%), and location (59%) in terms of a city or state.

The fact that most teenagers do not translate these online relationships into "real-life" relationships (Chan & Cheng, 2004; Cummings, Butler, & Kraut, 2002; Kraut, Butler, & Cumming, 2002) does not impair their function as alternative communities enabling sharing of different exposures on different levels. In her study on teenage Internet use, Sonia Livingstone (2008) interviewed 16 teenagers about their online behavior and found that they exhibited an intense interest in privacy. She found that the liveliest parts of the interview often had to do with the question of privacy: that is, what you show to others and what you keep private (Livingstone, 2008). She writes that:

> The teenagers described thoughtful decisions about what, how, and to whom they reveal personal information—drawing their own boundaries about what information to post or not, making deliberate choices that match their mode of communication (and its particular affordances) to particular communicative content. (Livingstone, 2008, p. 10)

This suggests that the teenagers defined privacy not only as the disclosure of certain types of information but instead, as having control over who knows what about you (Livingstone, 2006).

ISRAELI TEENAGE GIRL BLOGS: A CASE STUDY

Seventy-five percent of the bloggers on Israblog, the largest Hebrew-based blog platform (an equivalent of LiveJournal) are teenage girls. According to Israblog statistics, in August 2006, 74% of their total bloggers were minors and 73% were female (Vaisman, 2010a). From the outset of Israblog, the usage trend for female bloggers has been consistently upward, and by August 2010 had reached 78% (Vaisman, 2011).

It is additionally important to note major differences regarding privacy worries, between Israelis and Americans. Ribak and Turow (2003) found that Israelis were consistently more likely to agree that it was acceptable for a teenager to release certain types of information to marketers in exchange for a free gift. Americans confirmed to a much higher degree that their concerns about web privacy had increased since going online. The American parents were much more invested in the responsibility of government entities for controlling the web's power, and business responsibility "to be deeply involved in ensuring a web safe from teens' disclosure of information." Eighty-eight percent of the Americans, compared to only 43% of the Israelis, agreed strongly with the statement that they should know everything that a website knows about them, and this should be a legal right. Although Ribak and Turow did not study Israeli teenage girls' blogs, their finding that Israelis privacy perspectives do transfer to the Internet can be of aid when understanding the impact and expressions of and about privacy.

For this chapter, 50 weblogs written by Israeli teenage girls (aged 14–18 years old) were studied. The blog content was examined according to the privacy typology. Each type of exposure was analyzed according to five levels of exposure (an extra level was added specifically for this chapter).

Types of Exposure

- Factual (Personal) Exposure: Providing personal information and data, such as marital status, financial status, health condition, educational background and employment history, as well as biometric information and data, fingerprints, retinal scans, facial structure recognition and genetic information.
- Visual Exposure: Physical representation by means of photographs, revealing pictures of the body, video clips and so forth.
- Exposure of Identity and Emotions: Information about private opinions, viewpoints, feelings, principles, religious beliefs and personal characteristics.
- Exposure of Preferences: Individual consumer habits and preferences (with regard to merchandise, food, etc.)

Level of Exposure: (refers to all types of exposure)

- Level 1, Basic Familiarity: This level of exposure refers to basic information revealed during an initial introduction between two people, such as details about the place of residence, nationality, hobbies, etc.
- Level 2, Medium Familiarity: This level refers to information revealed between two personal acquaintances consistently over time, although not close friends. This includes references to the person's family, mood exposure and others.
- Level 3, High Familiarity: This level refers to the type of information revealed between close friends and family. It is defined by relatively high exposure of emotional and personal information, that is, intimate details, etc. It refers to behavior patterns that exist in the private sphere, and requires familiarity between people.
- Level 4, Intimate Familiarity: This level refers to the type of exposure that often occurs between spouses. This exposure level refers to behavior of a sexual nature, and relates to levels of emotional exposure and behavioral patterns generally relegated to the private sphere.
- Level 0, None: This level was included in this chapter only. This level refers to information that the author abstained from providing (leaving the rubric empty) or false information (revealing nothing in practice).

RESULTS

The findings revealed only the first three types of exposure in the teenage blogs. Furthermore, the authors distinguished between information provided on the blog feed and blog profile as well as between verbal and visual expressions (static or in motion).

The study found that many of the bloggers revealed factual (F) information in their blog profile section. For example, one blogger wrote, "me, "Jenni" / Yvgenya, Kiryat Gat (name of home town), 9th grade, and vegetarian" (F2).[1] The authors also found "add-on" text boxes, which were used as calling cards. For example, another blogger wrote, "Michal, almost 17, senior year . . . crazy, insane, jumpy, funny, creative, weird, shy, babbler, bored, lazy, loves food, 'loco,' hothead, cynical, childish, noisy, nice" (F3).[2] This is an example of factual exposure that indicates personality but not current feelings. Other examples of F exposure were found in the bloggers' feeds. For example, one blogger wrote, "I got wasted, it's the first time I've been so drunk . . . then one of the guys walked home with me so I wouldn't get hit by a car or something . . . that's how the night ended"(F3).[3] Another blogger, musing about her current situation, wrote, "The economic situation at home deteriorated this year, as for me the most important thing is that my father will find a good job, as a starter for this New Year."(F3).[4] Another type of high-level F exposure is one that reveals intimate information. For example, one blogger wrote "to" her mother: "I'm so angry with you! I think I started hating you when you told me you were cheating on dad, it's sad that after three years I found out you had three other men at that time, you slut!"[5] Many times such entries also featured other types of emotional (IE) exposure of feelings experienced in real time.

When it comes to emotional and personal (IE + VE) exposure, the study found that the teen bloggers expressed themselves in two forms: verbal and visual. Verbal expressions were divided into three groups: thoughts, insights and reflections. These included entries such as, "And I will never understand how this is always happening; she always has someone to be with (a guy) and I'm waiting on the side like a good dog."[6] Secondly, there is exposure of feelings and emotions in real time. For example, one blogger wrote, "Enoooough! I'm losing it here . . . finally I got over you, and tried going out with someone else. He is bullshitting me that he has a girlfriend and you're laughing in my face saying you were right—I'll never get to move on from you. So why do that to me? Be tight with your 'girlfriends' in my face, posting your pics with them? Fuck you. I've had enough of you."(IE4).[7] In this example the author is writing about how she feels in real time: she is "letting it all out."

A third type of exposure includes wishful thinking that reflects a momentary emotional outlet and not an actual plan or intention to follow. For example, "I'm sick of this life . . . sometimes I think I'll follow my sister (who actually did commit suicide). I hate everybody!!! My best friend stabs me in the back; my mom abuses my soul all day; my father is all she cares about, and I'm fucking all by myself!!!"(IE4).[8] "I'm exploding and on the verge of tears now. I don't have the strength for this life, private lessons, Yuvalim (excellence program), what a burden. I feel like I'm going to explode any second now. And will I do it next year? And the year after that? And then? I'll just kill myself"(IE3).[9]

Most of the types of IE and VE exposures were in the 3–4 familiarity level. However, there is a fourth type of exposure which includes statements, that is, pseudo-philosophical sayings indicating mood, temperament and beliefs. For example, one blogger wrote, "Why do all women want to be skinny? I fit my clothes to my body and not the other way around!"[10] Expressions of this sort appeared in the bloggers' profile as well in the lower levels 1–2, "Never share too many secrets"(IE1)[11] or "Never give up . . . You are stronger than you think" (IE2).[12]

Visual expressions are divided into three types of imaging: static (pictures, photos), mini moving-sequences that the girls find or edit themselves, and frames, static or moving, edited from popular TV shows including spoken text in subtitles. The authors appropriate the content as their personal expression. All of these images can stand alone or as sequels, creating a text. The level of exposure of each image was determined according to the following:

- VE0: Aesthetic elements with no emotional meaning, static or moving (like flowers, butterflies and such).
- VE1: Appears only in the profile and refers to the front page picture of the blog and its background. This image acts as an image statement, such as sexy anime figures, The Wall album cover, a hand holding a joint or images with pseudo-philosophical sayings like "We are slowly dying from the minute we are born."
- VE2: Literal visual expressions of the text, with no additional dimension or emotion. For example, a blogger writes "winter sucks" which is accompanied by a picture of a rainy window.
- VE3: Visuals bluntly reflecting text (usually in high levels of exposure) or visuals adding an interpretive element to the text. For example, a girl writes about wanting to cut her wrists and adds a visual of a bleeding hand (not hers).
- VE4: Blunt and explicit visuals that overshadow the actual text. For example, a blogger writes about her ex, "Pitz, I miss you" and this text is accompanied by a sequence of explicit pornographic visuals.

Visual Exposure (V)

This kind of exposure refers to personal photographs of the author, taken by her or of her. The four levels of exposure in this case are as follows:

- V1: Photographs taken by the author of cats, shopping (her purchases), scenery, and the like.
- V2: Personal passport-like pictures, making faces but nothing explicit or sexual. This level also shows family pictures, pictures taken with friends going out or in class and so on.
- V3: Pictures of the author alone, with a boyfriend or with her friends in more flirtatious and provocative poses. This includes kissing faces, revealing clothing, cleavage, and so on. This also includes pictures that seem innocent but are then revealed by the text to be "intimate" and not meant to be exposed publicly. For example, a blogger posts a photograph of a group of teenagers laughing and then reveals, through the text, that the teenagers are, in fact, high (under the influence of marijuana).
- V4: This level of exposure was not found in the research. This level of exposure refers to self-documentation of nudity, sex, explicit photos of

private parts or documentation of illegal actions like doing drugs, vandalism or violence.

The authors found four formulas of privacy. The highest level of privacy was reserved for the locked blogs, which require permission to read. Among the public blogs, the authors identified three categories of privacy: intimate/anonymous, identified and intermediate.

Intimate/Anonymous Blogs are characterized by high levels of 3–4 emotional (IE) and factual (F) exposure. Yet, for the most part, these blogs maintained high levels of author privacy and anonymity[13]—they usually have very limited profiles, sometimes completely empty, and maintain rigorous anonymity in their blog posts.[14] These blogs contain highly intimate information; the writing is very honest and revealing, emotionally and factually. There are almost no references to everyday issues beyond a reference to the event/events that triggered the emotional overflow being exposed in the blog. For example, in her blog, Walking Irony, the author writes, "Thanks a lot, for everything, really! I had such a great day, and you come and destroy it initially? It's so great how of all people, the ones closest to you can completely fuck up your day, in an hour. So thanks mom, thanks dad, thank you E, thank you A, thank you T, thank you for always knowing when the best moment is to ruin my mood."[15]

Having said that, some intimate blogs are not completely anonymous and identifying information can be found in the blog feed. However, a reading of the content indicates that the very existence of the blog is the secret, thus protecting the author's anonymity in the real world. One blogger explains, "Short opening, I've decided to change my blog name after stupidity took over and I accidentally told my best friend what it's called. So I really hope she did not get in here like she said she would and that she did not save it to her favorites list."[16] Me myself & I is even clearer about her expectations: "If you know me from real life it's a shame. Get out, fuck off and get lost!"[17] She also writes, "I am a 'Jerusalemite' and, like everybody else in the city, I'm completely anonymous. But if someone I know reads this, they'd recognize me."[18] She, and others like her, are aware of the fact that their feeds may reveal their true identity. For example, A Little Different asks/demands: "Hi, you know me from real life? You think you know who I am, who I'm talking about? Get out. Leave. Deny. Don't talk to me about it. Don't talk to others. Don't come back. It will only hurt me more."[19] In a different post, the same blogger realizes that her blog's anonymity has been breached: "I didn't mean it—I didn't mean for you to know. I didn't think you would find out. It's embarrassing that you know now. I don't want anyone to know. Don't want him to know. Don't want Kineret (girl's name) and the others to know. I don't want to know how and why they even know. I didn't want to know about her. I didn't want her to know. I don't want to know who else knows. But I know you've been reading. And I know you know and there's nothing to do. I didn't want this. But maybe now I do. And I'm not angry; it's public. I didn't mean for you to know. Maybe I didn't actually care? I don't know."[20]

In these blogs personal pictures are hardly ever found. In the rare case that they are, they do not provide any sort of revealing information. The authors of these blogs, at least intentionally, want them to be anonymous, honest and exposed while at the same time keeping their existence secret. As Saxonia explains in the first post of her current blog: "So . . . hi J my blog was discovered by people I know. So I started this one. WelcomeJ."[21] In contrast to personal photographs, the use of visual expressions of emotions (VE) at the higher levels of 3–4 is common to these blogs. For example, Walking Irony uploaded two edited scenes showing wrist cutting under the heading "Here we go again." At the end of the post she writes: "I'm tired of this feeling! I'm tired of crying so much for everything! I'm tired of living."[22]

The second category is the identified blogs. In these blogs the author does not hide who she is, knowingly and intentionally, even if she does not provide any identifying information in the blog's profile. These blogs contain many personal pictures, some of which are uploaded daily. The pictures are in the low—medium exposure levels, mostly 2 sometimes 3, and the factual and emotional exposure are about the same levels. The blog, A Girl with a Pearl Earring[23] is a good example of the first type of identified blogs. The author posts many pictures of herself accompanied by relatively intimate writing: "My ballet life in pictures and words—this post turned out to be huge and great—so this is my tenth year anniversary in classic ballet, in the same place with the same teacher, a fucking decade. So I want to record everything in pictures. Shall we?"[24] This post includes dozens of pictures, beginning with her childhood and progressing up to the present. Every picture is accompanied by an extended explanation regarding the relevant events and personal commentaries of the experience. In contrast, the blog No Brain No Worries is practically the author's visual diary. She uploads pictures of herself, of things she bought or made, of travels with her family and other daily events in the lower 2 visual and factual exposure levels. It is important to clarify that even though No Brain No Worries does not present intimate writing, she occasionally exposes level 3 information or emotions as well as pictures. The most important feature of identified blogs is that they reveal no intention to maintain the author's privacy.

A third category, which was rarely found in this research, is Intermediate Blogs. These blogs are characterized by detailed accounts of everyday life with a low level of exposure (level 2), with some moments of slightly higher exposure (level 3). For example, one blogger writes, "Final prep grades: 92 history, 88 grammar, 88 business; All that's left is the final exams, heeelp

(F2).[25] Yet another blogger writes: "Die, bitch, PLEASE! When you upload a photo of you smiling and write 'when she smiles everyone looks in her direction' I feel like writing 'maybe, but when you smile everybody looks away' but I won't, because you don't know I hate you" (IE3).[26] Another example is the blog 5 Good Things that Happened Today, which is dedicated to chronicling daily details: "I wrapped holiday gifts at the store . . . I did a fifth of my homework . . . I scored 1,000,000 in Temple Run, and this time, for real, since it is not April's 1st—I did not leave my house today which means I didn't need to wear makeup and my life is easier now."[27] Yet there are also a few that exhibit higher levels of exposure throughout. For example: "I was told that I'm pretty and look like a Barbie. I'm used to this Barbie thing, especially when I wear matching fuchsia pink lipstick and nail polish, but when it comes as a compliment it always makes me smile.[28] These blogs, while anonymous, lack the higher exposure levels that characterize the intimate blogs.

REFERENCES TO THE MEDIA

In general it seems that the bloggers view the blogosphere as an honest and authentic sphere, anonymous or not. The blog is a platform where they feel they can both demand and expect privacy: As Saxsonia (a blogger) writes, "First of all, it is really important that whoever recognizes him or herself in these posts stops reading immediately."[29] For many, the blog is a public-private place, where you expose and express yourself differently than in real life. Another blogger, Walking Irony explains: "I hate unloading my problems on people . . . my troubles. In a blog as you all will probably agree, it is much easier to do so because you are not face to face."[30] In a different post she explains: "A blog is a place for me to write everything in my heart and on my mind without being judged, right?"[31] In a similar vein, Not Just a Blonde expresses this point more clearly; in her profile, her blog is defined as a "refuge from life" and she pleads: "Did you identify me? Get out, let me know and don't say a thing. Don't come back here and don't tell anyone what is written here. Don't destroy the one place that is truly mine."[32]

The blogosphere is a sphere where one can demand privacy and respect the blog authors' anonymity. In contrast, Facebook is perceived as a public and exposed sphere where privacy and anonymity have no place, whereas the blog is a private and personal place that serves no social function.

This is why the demand for privacy and exposure in blogs is legitimate. More Than a Blonde argues that she shouldn't be criticized for any exposure made in her blog: "I don't care if you identify me. I thought about closing my blog or turning it 'private' because too many people from my class found out about it. However, I decided not to. If they're really important to me or if

I care about what they think, then I already told them about my blog, or they were nice enough to let me know they found it. (I hope so, I mean, if they don't tell me, they're just assholes and I don't care.) After all this is me, no masks or anything, the real me. I also have problems and complications and mistakes I have made; I'll probably make more. So I really don't care if you found out or identified me, but at least be decent enough to let me know you know my blog."[33] There are also some unique cases, like the post entitled "fucking eating disorder" by What For blog, where the author writes a very intimate post to a friend, in order for her to read it. In this way, the blog can also serve as a discreet platform for broadcasting intimate messages to a known recipient. What For writes: "You have ruined my best friend, (I know you're reading this, so know you're amazing with or without anorexia.) You have ruined her life, her health, her love for food. You have destroyed her soul, broken it, made her hate everything about herself . . ."[34]

Sometimes it seems that although the blog authors are aware that their blog is being read by many and that their posts are available in public in the blogosphere, they are not looking for popularity (followers), but rather for a small exclusive circle of confidants. For example, Strange Me expresses her fear of her blog becoming too popular: "Wow, to go into the blog statistics page and see 333 entrances a day in contrast to the previous 30–40 is crazy. Then to scroll down and find out it's all from the Israblog front page (landing page) . . . scary . . . I'm anonymous and really not into 'the more the better' as far as readers and followers."[35] In contrast, Facebook seems to be perceived as a place where you maintain and manage your social image. "Do you remember when we did not have Facebook but had a life? We used to take pictures to remember things and not to post to our wall,"[36] writes Saxsonia. April (another blogger) writes, "I've decided to limit my Facebook time. Why? Because it's all fake, corny and disgusting! It's repeating all the time. Statuses, pictures, likes, links and so . . . I have 500 friends . . . and it all feels so fake. I'm sick of all these clichés. People go to the mall with their friends and feel they need to upload pictures of themselves to prove that their lives are fun and exciting . . . and then there are the pathetic ones who ask for "likes"(i.e., give me a "like" and I'll give you one back) . . . what da'fuck? It's so obvious, stop adding people you don't know just to have more pics on your wall, so everyone can see how many friends you've got."

These findings echo Dalsgaard's (2008) research which identified that the main feature of information uploaded to Facebook is that it deals with social interaction and activities and not with individual personal issues. With Facebook, an individual's social image is comprised of the number of "friends" one has and the social interactions one records and not by the amount of personal information he reveals. The negative references to Facebook are also interesting. As No Brain No Worries explains: "First post, first draft—I wonder what made me do this . . . What was the thing that made me wish to share and unload the burden of my life. What pushed me to leave the mainstream and reach for the alternative? I have 700 friends on Facebook and none of them is actually a friend."[37] Mainstream here means available to everyone, not challenging and not unique. She adds "I feel that this [the blog] is my only refuge. My shelter from the world; some kind of parallel universe where I can pour my heart out, a place where I won't be judged."[38]

SUMMARY

Privacy for Attention

In recent years, blogs have become increasingly used by adolescent girls as a tool for personality and identity formation as a means of expressing their independence and exploring their relationship to the world. The "personal diaries" used by generations of young girls and women to document their personal, intimate experiences behind lock and key, hidden from the eyes of their family members, have assumed a new form and new nature. The key principle of "writing to yourself" has disappeared. Gone is the writing as a type of personal therapy, a desire to remember events and retain memories, or a place where you can fully express yourself to yourself. The blog format blurs these goals when the author develops an awareness, however slight, that he/she has an audience.

Blogs, one of the most prominent illustrations of the transformation of the concept of privacy, effectively represent the intersection of privacy and "publicness." In some respects, blogs are still at an intermediary stage: Physically, a blog takes place in the privacy of a young girl's bedroom, but it is intended for public consumption in virtual cyberspace. The bedroom walls of privacy obliterate the awareness of the publicness of cyberspace. "The medium is the message," said Mcluhan (1964), and he is correct. Web technology has changed the nature of "journals" and adolescent girls' fundamental attitude toward their journals. These changes are also manifested in the journal's physical format: While the journal of the past was based mainly on personal writing, the blog contains the variety of images that represent the types of visual exposure that the young girl wishes to reveal to the world. These images include photos captured by the blogger, personal images in which she appears alone or with others, with partners or friends, in innocent and in sexual or physically explicit contexts.

In the Internet era, images have become a popular, accessible means of expression and communication, and it is not surprising that they have become one of the components of exposure used in blogs. An analysis of blogs illustrates the process described in this book, characterizing adolescent girls and their desire to be seen, which increasingly supplants the former desire for privacy.

Within our study, three main types of exposure was founded: On "personal blogs," the girls fully expose their emotional and factual selves, but maintain visual privacy. They write explicitly about themselves and their emotions, yet at the same time make an effort to protect their anonymity. The information in their profiles range from sparse to non existent, and they may even turn directly to their readers and ask them to stop reading the blog if they are able to identify its author. Such an approach reveals the author's desire to remain anonymous despite her awareness of the "risk" of exposure. This risk of exposure is also appealing, as Little Different explains to her friends: She knows that her friends will read her blog and she doesn't want them to, but she then writes, "Now maybe I do want them to read it." This example illustrates the barometer-like function of blogs: Blogs can be used to test the temperature of the water before plunging head first into the pool. Bloggers post their entries anonymously, sending out feelers for responses. If the responses are favorable, the blogger can surmise that exposure will be beneficial.

The second type of blog is "identified blogs," in which the bloggers make no effort to conceal their identity. On the contrary, bloggers upload personal images that reveal their appearance, clearly signaling that they do not wish to remain anonymous. Blog entries disclose relatively intimate details of their lives and past, and describe events from their everyday lives in detail. The images the bloggers upload from their past and present are accompanied by their explanations and interpretations, creating a comprehensive layer of exposure. In blogs of this type, bloggers are not interested in maintaining anonymity; just the opposite: these girls seek exposure, as illustrated by the photographed journal of No Mind No Worries. The photos document her and her actions in her everyday life. The typical feature of these blogs is the bloggers' desire for exposure and the desire to be seen.

Moreover, in the new media era, where blogging can be done by any platform, the opportunity of being exposed is getting bigger. For example, Tumblr, a publishing platform, enables the user to create his own personal blog just by giving his e-mail account (Aamoth, 2013). The instant-blogging that the app created encouraged thousands of people to expose every part of their day, through their cell phones. The online publishing editor in Tumblr has templates to create and share regular text posts, videos, photos, quotes, audio files, chat logs and links. All of these features also helped motivating users to share and expose others to intimate situations happening in their lives. The significant amount of registered users is again raising the question of privacy boundaries, which are reshaped by users who seek to be shown and voluntarily expose themselves.

The third type of blogs, which accounted for a relatively small group in our sample, is the hybrid format. In this category, as seen, bloggers who reveal significant details of their private lives, including very explicit emotional exposure, yet maintain some degree of anonymity. The anonymity character-istic of hybrid blogs is more limited than the anonymity typical of "personal" bloggers, and contains visual cues of varying levels of exposure. The key feature of hybrid blogs is, however, their interactivity and the authors' interactions with their audience: The bloggers actively address the audience, solicit comments and feedback, and correspond with their readers. They wish to publish and be visible; theirs is a desire to be present, to elicit responses, as a validation of their own existence. These bloggers need the mirror held by their audience, their readers, and others, in order to develop their own sense of identity.

In all three types of blogs, the bloggers share a complex relationship with their audience. Their writing is accompanied by a slight, partial or strong desire for exposure, and they repeatedly address this desire in various ways. The girls develop partial awareness of their audience—who are sometimes known to them and sometimes anonymous. If privacy is the right to control the information that others know about us, then these girls occasionally seek to conceal information from people close to them, including their parents and teachers, and sometimes even from their friends at school or in youth move-ments, while simultaneously exposing themselves to mass audiences, feeling like celebrities. They seek to attract as many random readers as possible while reducing the risk of attracting people who actually know them in real life.

The known or anonymous audience that reads the blogposts constitutes a certain power and influence, and references to such audiences reflects an interesting situation of the bloggers' simultaneous awareness and denial of their "presence." This new blog privacy still makes "false awareness" pos-sible, making it possible for bloggers to hold an illusionary belief of the situ-ation. We want to be seen but also want to control who the viewers will be. We want the audience's love and affirmation, but expect to be able to select the audience and affect it, as Saxsonia stated, "If you are mentioned in the next section, please stop reading." This type of request or demand stresses the bloggers' dual expectations of privacy and its anticipated violation. Their desire for exposure without the anticipated judgmental responses in every-day life goes hand in hand with the desire for understanding, sympathy or legitimacy.

As Huffacker (2006) argues, the desire for love and the ability to reveal genuine emotions is sometimes easier to accomplish with strangers than with people closest to you.

At the same time, these blogs are also intimate spaces from which the blog-gers address familiar friends directly, stating things they cannot reveal in person. As we have seen, blogs are considered the space that hosts interactions that are more genuine than those in real life, the space where the "true" things are said or written, whether they are direct to a specific individual or to virtual friends. When What For addresses her friends directly and writes that she knows that they ruined her best friend's life and adds in parentheses that she knows that her friend is reading her blog—she is using her blog as a type of medium that is not possible in real life. The distance between addresser and addressee that the blog creates facilitates the disclosure of information and expression of more candid and intimate messages.

In contrast to Facebook, where the young adolescent girl presents her "most wonderful" self, the blog is a portrayal of her "aching" self. On her blog, the adolescent girl discusses her problems with her family, friends, school and other life issues that concern her. She does this while constructing a personality and identity that can shift along the continuum from anonymity to exposure. Bloggers distinguish between FB and the blogosphere: FB is considered an exposed arena where the adolescent girl fashions the image she wishes to project to the world, a wonderful, idealized self. This self is portrayed to numerous others with whom she maintains relationships that are superficial, fake and even hypocritical.

Her blog, in contrast, is where genuine feelings, true stories, and personal photos are revealed, and where privacy is a legitimate demand. Privacy is also implicated by the distinct intentions in these two platforms: When you stage your visible self for the world, you are not entitled to privacy: What you want and what you are entitled to is attention. But when you express your true, painful and not necessarily attractive emotions, you are entitled to privacy. This distinction emphasizes the transitional stage of these blogs— the stage at which the Internet seems to be a private, controllable space that "is considerate" of the author's intentions. However, as we see in the next chapter, the Internet is not that kind of space at all. It is where there are almost no limits to people's desire to penetrate the personal spaces of others.

A major feature of the Internet is its potential to create a community of people who share interests and assist each other in obtaining information, sharing advice, impressions, emotions, photos and facts. More than anything, being a blogger allows the individual to belong to such a community—a community of bloggers. This community may be anonymous but it comprises authors who share the identity of bloggers. This community is also known in the literature as a peer community, based on bloggers' sense of belonging to a community in which members are equal (Brown, 1983; Damon, 2004a). The singularity of such groups is that members are not necessarily identified by the details of their everyday lives, but rather on the basis of the identities they created for themselves online. These new identities seek attention.

The privacy of the past that was entirely one's own has become replaced by a desire for attention—sometimes what is sought is a distinct kind of attention, but it still is based on visibility to others. This creates a combination of the desire for varying degrees of exposure and anonymity, and the desire to belong to a community—a brotherhood. In our study, adolescent girls feel that the image they project in their blogs is genuine and honest and not invented. They seek the responses of their audience specifically on the basis of this honesty. The attention they seek is designed for empowerment and reinforcement, as illustrated by Sample 63 who received many "amazing" responses and gained a sense of identification and support from her community.

The chapter demonstrates how blogs are enabling Israeli adolescents to feel part of a community. Belonging to a community is one of the strongest features of adolescence: adolescents have always wanted to be popular, loved, and part of the gang. This is true for people in general, but the desire to be cradled by a community is intensified during adolescence, when we develop our sense of identity through the people with whom we associate and the groups to which we belong. In the past, we carefully protected our privacy and wrote our deepest secrets for our own eyes only, for our desk drawer. We tended to project a different image to those close to us versus more remote individuals. We felt that we could be our true selves only with the people closest to us.

This book demonstrates that the media is pointing in a different direction—in order to be part of a community and fit it, we can remove our disguise and allow others to observe us, get to know us, and follow us, almost limitlessly. Such exposure is the means for gaining recognition and love. We can be part of a group or community, whether it is a group of bloggers, and group of people we know, or a group of entirely unknown people. Our desire and need for belonging expands our boundaries, and our private lives and selves are no longer revealed only to those close to us. Virtuality allows a broader embrace and greater love than before, but privacy undermines this type of support. The fear of emotional, visual or factual exposure limits the potential embrace and broad attention that the virtual world offers. Stalking as a type of intimidation has become a source of appeal for adolescents and a source of validation: follow me to see me, to prove that I exist.

NOTES

1. Jeni, http://israblog.nana10.co.il/blogread.asp?blog=813938&blogcode=13443225.

2. Michal, http://israblog.nana10.co.il/blogread.asp?blog=749443.

3. Girl with a Pearl Earring, http://israblog.nana10.co.il/blogread.asp?blog=8047 81&year=2012&month=5.

4. Derpina, 1/1/2012 02:35 sample 378.

5. Sample 989What for? 19/9/2012 20:27.

6. Derpina, http://israblog.nana10.co.il/blogread.asp?blog=652205&year=2012 &month=1.

7. Shirrooos http://israblog.nana10.co.il/blogread.asp?blog=813680.

8. Lee_09, http://israblog.nana10.co.il/blogread.asp?blog=815565.

9. Nic, http://israblog.nana10.co.il/blogread.asp?blog=814313&year=2012&mo nth=7.

10. Girl with a Pearl Earring, http://israblog.nana10.co.il/blogread.asp?blog=8047 81&year=2012&month=5.

11. McQueen, http://israblog.nana10.co.il/blogread.asp?blog=745015.

12. Nana6, http://israblog.nana10.co.il/blogread.asp?blog=767052.

13. Lee_09, http://israblog.nana10.co.il/blogread.asp?blog=815565.

14. April Blog AL, http://israblog.nana10.co.il/blogread.asp?blog=689795.

15. Walking Irony, http://israblog.nana10.co.il/blogread.asp?blog=813618&year= 2012&month=4.

16. Amasiar, http://israblog.nana10.co.il/blogread.asp?blog=762904&year=2011 &month=9.

17. Me Myself & I, http://israblog.nana10.co.il/blogread.asp?blog=816988.

18. Fascinating, http://israblog.nana10.co.il/blogread.asp?blog=808892&blogc ode=13405331.

19. Katzarehet, http://israblog.nana10.co.il/blogread.asp?blog=816478.

20. Katzarehet, http://israblog.nana10.co.il/blogread.asp?blog=816478.

21. Saxonia, http://israblog.nana10.co.il/blogread.asp?blog=753759&blogc ode=13427082.

22. Walking Irony, http://israblog.nana10.co.il/blogread.asp?blog=813618&year= 2012&month=4.

23. Derpina, http://israblog.nana10.co.il/blogread.asp?blog=652205&year=2012 &month=1.

24. Girl with a Pearl Earring, http://israblog.nana10.co.il/blogread.asp?blog=8047 81&year=2012&month=5.

25. Wicked Mind, http://israblog.nana10.co.il/blogread.asp?blog=805681&year=2 012&month=9.

26. Wicked Mind, http://israblog.nana10.co.il/blogread.asp?blog=805681&year=2 012&month=9.

27. 5 good things that happened to me today, http://israblog.nana10.co.il/blogread. asp?blog=758248&year=2012&month=4.

28. 5 good things that happened to me today, http://israblog.nana10.co.il/blogread. asp?blog=758248&year=2012&month=4.

29. Saxonia, http://israblog.nana10.co.il/blogread.asp?blog=753759&blogcode= 13427082.

30. Walking Irony, http://israblog.nana10.co.il/blogread.asp?blog=813618&year= 2012&month=4.

31. Walking Irony, http://israblog.nana10.co.il/blogread.asp?blog=813618&year=2012&month=4.

32. Not just a blonde, http://israblog.nana10.co.il/blogread.asp?blog=808400&year=2012&month=6.

33. Not just a blonde, http://israblog.nana10.co.il/blogread.asp?blog=808400&year=2012&month=6.

34. What for?, http://israblog.nana10.co.il/blogread.asp?blog=816553.

35. Strange me, http://israblog.nana10.co.il/blogread.asp?blog=814599&year=2012&month=7.

36. Saxonia, http://israblog.nana10.co.il/blogread.asp?blog=753759&blogcode=13427082.

37. No sheckels no worries http://israblog.nana10.co.il/blogread.asp?blog=805147&catcode=&year=2012&month=8&day=0&pagenum=3&catdesc.

38. No sheckels no worries, http://israblog.nana10.co.il/blogread.asp?blog=805147&catcode=&year=2012&month=8&day=0&pagenum=3&catdesc.

REFERENCES

Aamoth, D. (2013, May 19). What is Tumblr. *Time Online*. Retrieved from http://techland.time.com/2013/05/19/what-is-tumblr/.

Adar, E., & Adamic, L.A. (2005). Tracking information epidemics in blogspace. *Proceedings of the 2005 IEEE/WIC/ ACM International Joint Conference on Web Intelligence and Intelligent Agent Technology*, Compiègne, France, September 19–22.

Aharony, N. (2009). Librarians and information scientists in the blogosphere: An exploratory analysis. *Library & Information Science Research, 31*, 174–181. doi: 10.1016/j.lisr.2009.02.001.

Ali-Hasan, N.F., & Adamic, L.A. (2007). Expressing social relationships on the blog through links and comments. *Proceedings of International Conference on Weblogs and Social Media*, Boulder, CO, March 26–28.

Anderson, R.E. (2002). Youth and information technology. In J. Mortimor & R. Larson (Eds.), *The future of adolescent experience: Societal trends and the transition to adulthood* (pp. 175–207). New York: Cambridge University Press.

Becker, J.A.H. & Stamp, G.H. (2005). Impression management in chat rooms: A grounded theory model. *Communication Studies, 56*, 243–260.

Benson, A. & Favini, R. (2006). Evolving the Web, evolving librarian. *Library Hi Tech News 23*(7) 2006, 18–21.

Blood, R. (2000, September 7). Weblogs: A history and perspective. http://www.rebeccablood.net/essays/weblog_history.html.

Blood, R. (2002a). *The weblog handbook: Practical advice on creating and maintaining your blog*. Cambridge, MA: Perseus Publishing.

Blood, R. (2002b). Introduction. In J. Rodzvilla (ed.), *We've got blog: How weblogs are changing our culture* (pp. ix–xii). Cambridge, MA: Perseus Publishing.

Blood, R. (2004). How blogging software reshapes the online community. *Communications of the ACM, 47*(12), pp. 53–55.

Bortree, D.S. (2005). Presentation of self on the web: An ethnographic study of teenage girls' Weblogs. *Education, Communication & Information, 5*, 25–39.

Boyd, D. (2007). Why youth heart? Social network sites: The role of networked publics in teenage social life. In D. Buckingham (Ed.), *Youth, identity, and digital media* (pp. 119–142). Cambridge, MA: MIT Press.

Boyd, D. (2008). Taken out of context: American teen sociality in networked publics. Unpublished dissertation. Retrieved September 23, 2014, from http://www.danah. org/papers/TakenOutOfContext.pdf.

Boyd, D. (2014). *It's complicated: The social lives of networked teens.* New Haven, CT: Yale University Press.

Brown, B.B. (2004). Adolescents' relationships with peers. In R.M. Lerner & L. Steinberg (Eds.), *Handbook of adolescents' psychology* (2nd ed., pp. 363–394). Hoboken, NJ: John Wiley and Sons.

Cadle, L. (2005). A public view of private writing: Personal weblogs and adolescent girls, *Dissertation Abstracts International, Section A: The Humanities and Social Sciences*, (4) 2005 October, 1342. Bowling Green State U, 2005. DA3171254.

Calvert, S.L., Jordan, A.B., & Cocking, R.R. (Eds.). (2002). *Children in the digital age: Influences of electronic media on development.* Westport, CT: Praeger.

Chan, D.K.S. & Cheng, G.H.L. (2004). Offline and online friendship qualities at different stages of relationship development. *Journal of Social and Personal Relationships, 21*, 305.

Chau, M., & Xu, J. (2012). Business intelligence in blogs: Understanding consumer interactions and communities. *MIS Quarterly, 36*(4), 1189–1216.

Cheng, G.H.-L. (2004). A comparison of offline and online friendship quality at different stages of relationship development. *Journal of Social and Personal Relationships, 21*(3), 305–320.

Child, J.T., Pearson, J.C., & Petronio, S. (2009). Blogging, communication, and privacy management: Development of the blogging privacy management measure. *Journal of the American Society For Information Science & Technology, 60*(10), 2079–2094. doi:10.1002/asi.21122.

Chittenden, T, (2010). Digital dressing up: Modelling female teen identity in the discursive spaces of the fashion blogosphere. *Journal of Youth Studies, 13*, 505–508.

Cummings, J., Butler, B., & Kraut, R. (2002). The quality of online social relationships. *Communications of the ACM, 45*(7), 103–108.

Calvert, S.L., Jordan, A.B., & Cocking, R.R. (Eds.). (2002). *Children in the digital age: Influences of electronic media on development.*Westport, CT: Praeger.

Dalsgaard S., (2008). Facework on Facebook: The presentation of self in virtual life and its role in the US elections. *Anthropology Today, 24*(6), 8–12, December 2008.

Davis, K. (2010). Coming of age online: The developmental underpinnings of girls' blogs. *Journal of Adolescent Research, 25*(1), 145–171. doi:10.1177/074355840 9350503

Erikson, E. (1963). *Childhood and society.* New York: WW Norton & Company.

Festa, P. (2003, February 25). Blogging comes to Harvard. *CNET News.com.* http://news.com.com/2008–1082-985714.html?tag=fd_nc_1.

García-Gómez, A. (2009). Teenage girls' personal weblog writing. *Information, Communication & Society, 12*(5), 611–638. doi:10.1080/13691180802266657.

Gilbert, P. (1995). On space, sex and stalkers. *Women and Performance, 17*, 1–18.

Gill, A.J., Nowson, S., & Oberlander, J. (2009, May). What are they blogging about? Personality, topic and motivation in blogs. In the *International Conference on Weblogs and Social Media.*

Goffman, E. (1959 [1990]). *The presentation of self in everyday life.* London: Penguin Books.

Graham, C., M. Rouncefield, & C. Satchell. (2009). Blogging as 'therapy'? Exploring personal technologies for smoking cessation. *Health Informatics Journal 15*: 267–281. doi:10.1177/1460458209345897.

Gross, E. (2004). Adolescent Internet use: What we expect, what teens report. *Journal of Applied Developmental Psychology, 25*, 633–649.

Gruhl, D., Guha, R., Liben-Nowell, D., & Tomkins, A. (2004). Information diffusion through Blogspace. *Proceedings of the 13th International World Wide Web Conference, New York*, May 17–20, pp. 491–501.

Gunter, B. (2008) Blogging: Private becomes public and public becomes personalised. *Aslib Proceedings, Special Issue: Blogging and the Erosion of Public and Private Life Spheres, 61*(2), 120–126.

Haas, A., Blair, K., & Tulley, C. (2002). Mentors versus master: Women's and girls' narratives of (re)negotiation in web-based writing spaces. *Computers and Composition, 19*(3), 231–249.

Herring, S.C. (2000). Gender differences in CMC: Findings and implications. *Computer Professionals for Social Responsibility Journal, 18*(1). Retrieved from http://cpsr.org/issues/womenintech/herring/ (14 April 2009).

Herring, S. (2001). Computer-mediated discourse. In D. Schiffrin, D. Tannen & H. Hamilton (Eds.), *Handbook of discourse analysis* (pp. 612–634). Blackwell Publishers: Oxford.

Herring, S.C., Scheidt, L.A., Bonus, S., & Wright, E. (2005). Weblogs as a bridging genre. *Information, Technology, & People, 18*(2), 142–171.

Hollenbaugh, E.E. & Everett, M.K. (2013). The effects of anonymity on self-disclosure in blogs: An application of the online disinhibition effect. *Journal of Computer-Mediated Communication 18*, 283–302.

Hollenbaugh, E.E. (2011). Motives for maintaining personal journal blogs. *Cyberpsychology, Behavior & Social Networking, 14*(1/2), 13–20. doi:10.1089/cyber.2009.0403.

Huffaker, D.A., & Calvert, S.L. (2005). Gender, identity, and language use in teenage blogs. *Journal of Computer-Mediated Communication, 10*(2), Retrieved April 2013. http://jcmc.indiana.edu/vol10/issue2/huffaker.html.

Huffaker, D. (2006). Teen blogs exposed: The private lives of teens made public. *Presented at the American Association for the Advancement of Science (AAAS) in* St. Louis, MO. February 16–19.

Kraut, R.E., Butler, B.S., & Cummings, J. (2002). The quality of social ties online. *Communication of the ACM*, 47(7), 103–108.

Kuhn, M. (2007). A code of blogging ethics: Interactivity and prioritizing the human. *Journal of Mass Media Ethics: Exploring Questions of Media Morality 22*, 37–41.

Kumar, R., Novak, J., Raghavan, P., & Tomkins, A. (2005). On the bursty evolution of blogspace. *World Wide Web: Internet and Web Information Systems* (8), pp. 159–178.

Lee, C.M., Bates, J.A. (2007). Mapping the Irish biblioblogosphere: Use and perceptions of library weblogs by Irish librarians. *The Electronic Library, 25*(6), 648–663.

Lenhart, A., Purcell, K., Smith, A., & Zickuhr, K. (2010). *Social media & mobile internet use among teens and young adults*. Washington D.C.: Pew Internet & American Life Project. Retrieved from http://files.eric.ed.gov/fulltext/ED525056.pdf.

Lenhart, A., Madden, M., & Hitlin, P. (2005). *Teens and technology: Youth are leading the transition to a fully wired and mobile nation*. Washington D.C.:PEW Internet and Family Life.

Lenhart, A., Rainie, L., & Lewis, O. (2001). *Teenage life online: The rise of the instant message generation and the internet's impact on friendships and family relationships*. Washington D.C.: Pew Internet & American Life Project.

Lin, C.L., & Kao, H.Y. (2010). Blog popularity mining using social interconnection analysis. *IEEE Internet Computing Magazine, 14*(4), 41–49.

Livingstone, S., & Bober, M. (2005). *UK children go online: Final report of key project findings*. London: Economic and Social Research Council (eSociety).

Livingstone, S. (2008). Taking risky opportunities in youthful content creation: Teenagers' use of social networking sites for intimacy, privacy and self-expression. *New Media & Society, 10*(3). 393–411.

Lövheim, M. (2011). Young women's blogs as ethical spaces. *Information, Communication & Society, 14*(3), 338–354.

Mayer-Schönberger, V., (2011). *Delete: The virtue of forgetting in the digital age*. Woodstock, Oxfordshire, UK: Princeton University Press.

McCullagh, K. (2008). Blogging: Self presentation and privacy. *Information & Communications Technology Law, 17*(1), 3–23. doi:10.1080/13600830801886984.

Nahon, K., Hemsley, J., Walker, S., & Hussain, M. (2011). Blogs: Spinning a web of virality. *Proceedings of the iConference*, Seattle, WA, February 8–11.

Nardi, B., Schiano, D., & Gumbrecht, M. (2004). Blogging as social activity, or, would you let 900 million people read your diary? *Proceedings of Computer Supported Cooperative Work [2004 online]*. Retrieved from: http://home.comcast.net/diane.schiano/CSCW04.Blog.pdf [Accessed 1 September 2014].

Nowson, S., & Oberlander J. (2006). The identity of bloggers: Openness and gender in personal weblogs. Presented at *AAAI Spring Symposium, Computational Approaches to Analysing Weblogs*, Stanford University. Retrieved from: http://www.aaai.org/Papers/Symposia/Spring/2006/SS-06–03/SS06-03-032.pdf.

Nurmi, J.-E. (2004). Socialization and self-development: Channeling, selection, adjustment and reflection. In R.M. Lerner & L. Steinberg (Eds.), *Handbook of adolescent psychology* (2nd ed., pp. 85–124). Hoboken, New Jersey: John Wiley & Sons.

Paechter, C. (2013). Young women online: Collaboratively constructing identities. *Pedagogy, Culture and Society, 21*, 111–127. doi:10.1080/14681366.2012.748684.

Palfrey, J., & Glasser, U. (2008). *Born digital: Understanding the first generation of digital natives.* New York: Basic Books.

Parsad, B., & Jones, J. (2005). *Internet access in U.S. public schools and classrooms: 1994–2003.* Washington D.C.: National Center Education Statistics.

Qian, H., & Scott, C.R. (2007). Anonymity and self-disclosure on weblogs. *Journal of Computer-Mediated Communication, 12*(4), 1428–1451. Retrieved March 25, 2009, From http://jcmc.indiana.edu/vol12/issue4/qian.html.

Rainie, L., & Hitlin, P. (2005). *The internet at school.* Washington D.C.: PEW Internet and American Life.

Rainie, L., & Horrigan, J. (2005). *How the internet has woven itself into American life.* Washington D.C.: PEW Internet and Family Life Project.

Ribak, R., & Turow, J. (2003). Internet power and social context: A globalization approach to Web privacy concerns. *Journal of Broadcasting & Electronic Media, 47*(3), 328–349.

Rideout, V., Roberts, D.F., & Foehr, U.G. (2005). *Generation M: Media in the lives of 8–18 year-olds.* Washington D.C.: Kaiser Family Foundation.

Sanderson, J., & Kassing, J.W. (2011). Tweets and blogs: Transformative, adversarial, and integrative developments in sports media. In A.C. Billings (Ed.), *Sports media: Transformation, integration, consumption* (pp. 114–127). New York: Routledge.

Schiano, D.J., Nardi, B.A., Gumbrecht, M., & Swartz, L. (2004, May). Blogging by the rest of us. *Proceedings of CHI 2004.* Vienna, Austria.

Sinanan, J., Graham, C., & Jie, K.Z. (2014). Crafted assemblage: Young women's 'lifestyle' blogs, consumerism and citizenship in Singapore, *Visual Studies, 29*(2), 201–213, DOI:10.1080/1472586X.2014.887273.

Stefanone, M.A., & Chyng-Yang, J. (2007). Writing for friends and family: The interpersonal nature of blogs. *Journal of Computer-Mediated Communication, 13*(1), 123–140. doi:10.1111/j.1083–6101.2007.00389.x.

Stern, S. (2007). Producing sites, exploring identities: Youth online authorship. In D. Buckingham (Ed.), *Youth, identity, and digital media* (pp. 95–117). Cambridge, MA: MIT Press

Takayoshy, P. (2000). Complicated women: Examining methodologies for understanding the uses of technology. *Computers and Composition, 17,* 123–138.

"2013 Digital Influence Report." Technorati. Retrieved from: http://technorati.com/report/2013-dir/

Tice, D.M., Butler, J.L., Muraven, M.B., & Stillwell, A.M. (1995). When modesty prevails: Differential favorability of self-presentation to friends and strangers. *Journal of Personality and Social Psychology, 69,* 1120–1138.

Vaisman, C.L. (2011). So fun, muy kef: Lexical glocalization in Israeli girls' blogs. *Israel Studies in Language and Society 4*(1).

Viegas, F.B. (2005). Bloggers' expectations of privacy and accountability: An initial survey. *Journal of Computer-Mediated Communication,* 10(3), article 12. Retrieved from http://jcmc.indiana.edu/vol10/issue3/vieacutegas.html.

Winer, D. (1999). The history of weblogs. http://newhome.weblogs.com/history of Weblogs.

Winer, D. (2001, November 16). What are weblogs? http://newhome.weblogs.com/personalWebPublishingCommunities.

Chapter 6

Popularity in Your Pocket

Your Private Self Exposed on Your Mobile Phone

Trying to examine and understand privacy exposure is almost impossible without a thorough examination of mobile phones, which have drastically changed our notions of the personal and private space. In their book *Perpetual Contact: Mobile Communication, Private Talk, Public Performance*, which was published before the invention of the smartphone, James E. Katz and Mark Aakhus (2002) highlighted the dependency of modern mankind on the mobile phone stating how "over the years, the telephone has dramatically changed how people live their lives and see their world" (Schezter & Cohen, in: Katz, Aakhus 2002, p. 38).

Cui, Chipchase and Ichikawa (2007) argue that the mobile phone is a ubiquitous information and communication tool. Today, for many people the mobile phone is the first thing that they interact with in the morning, and one of the last objects they use before going to sleep at night. The mobile is typically used in almost every context in between (Chipchase, J. et al., 2005).

Shin Dong Kim (2000) has found that people who use mobile phones have a stronger tendency toward collectivity and an active social life at the expense of private life, insinuating weak boundaries between their social and private lives. Kim gives a variety of examples he has encountered which demonstrate how the line between the public and private spheres is blurred for mobile users: For example, a woman talking about intimate subjects on her mobile phone sitting in the subway train, without noticing nor caring that strangers are listening (Shin Dong Kim, 2000).

BIRTH OF THE MOBILE PHONE

Although the first mobile connection was made in the 1970s, it was not until the twenty-first century that the device began to significantly influence the way people interact. The "cellular culture" as defined by Gerard Goggin (2006) was officially inaugurated when the mobile phone became more easily accessible to a significant number of people around the world. When reviewing the technological changes in mobile phones, the 1980s are considered the period when the classic form of the mobile phone was stabilized. It was the decisive shift to a stand-alone portable telephone which provided the material basis for a set of new design features that are now regarded as standard for mobile phones (Googin, 2006, p. 1).

According to Fortunati (2006), the beginning of the dramatic change happened in the 1990s when the second-generation digital mobile system became dominant and reshaped the technological-cultural atmosphere. Mobile phones became smaller, more portable, and domestic. They became part of our everyday lives and this was accompanied by the inclusion of new features, capabilities and communicative architectures, as well as cultural expectations and routines—all in this pocket-sized technology (Goggin, 2009). These technological changes hastened the death of privacy as we know it and reshaped our grasp of its cultural boundaries (Den Hoven, 2008).

Goggin (2006) contends that the power of mobile phones was unclear at the beginning of the century. However, their rapid influence quickly transformed them from a simple voice call instrument to an essential tool for everyday life. Therefore, when reviewing current literature about the implications of mobile phones within our lives, the image of cellular domination is clear. Many scholars have conducted comprehensive studies tracing differences in mobile phone use. In one study, Hossein, Falaki and colleagues (2010) examined 255 mobile phone users and found that the average number of mobile phone interactions per day varied from 10 to 200, and the average amount of data received per day varied from 1 to 1000 MB. Once comprehending the magnitude of the daily consumption and exposure involved, we begin to realize the remarkable growth in mobile phone usage.

Mobile Phone Usage in Israel

Before being able to understand mobile phone practices in Israel, it is important to illustrate the shift that has occurred in Israeli society over the decades. Although Israel has long been transformed into a liberal capitalist state, it was founded on strong collective roots and a history of similar experiences and common frameworks among a significant portion of its citizens. The Zionist identity is collectivist in principle, distinguished by particular aspects (secular or religious Jews) and universal values such as socialism and nationalism (Kimmerling & Moore, 1997). The *sabra* generation, the first generation of Jews who were educated in the Jewish settlements of Palestine, were assimilated and socialized in social-communal institutions, including the kibbutz, the moshav, youth movements, pre-military corps, and others (Almog, 2000). *Sabras* later achieved political hegemony in the formative years of the new Israeli society, from 1930 to 1960. The cultural arena focused mainly on amplifying the power of this group and its ideals and missions, as indicated in Almog's (2000) findings, based on popular childrens' and teenage literature of the period. This may explain the somewhat paradoxical character of Israeli society. On the one hand, Israelis have embraced the values of individualism, liberty and freedom, but on the other, they continue to hold the collective ethos of community sharing and belonging (Ribak, 2007). This strong sense of community sharing and belonging is salient in the realm of media and technology, and is especially notable considering the personal exposure demonstrated in mobile phone practices among Israelis. Technology has created a new need, a need that naturally makes us want to expose and/or to be exposed, as exemplified below.

When examining the local perspective of mobile phone usage, Katz and Aakhus (2002) noted that the rate of mobile phone adoption in Israel was rapid and profound. They have claimed that Israelis harbor the following characteristics that make them more attached to their mobile phones: (1) they are very fond of communication technology (2) they have a significant need to be socially connected and (3) mobility and rapid information fits their temperament (Schezter & Cohen, as quoted in Katz, Aakhus 2002).

By the end of 2011, there were an estimated 1,055,000 mobile subscribers in Israel, representing a growth of 1.5% over the year and a mobile penetration rate of 133% (Hatuka & Toch, 2014). In their study on mobile phone usage and its impact on social interactions, Hatuka and Toch (2014) asked how the temporary disregard of one's physical environment (mainly, the people around us) while using a smartphone influences the social interactions in a place. How does this dynamic shape behavior in public spaces?

The researchers explored the practices and actions of subjects in public spaces during March–May 2011 at Tel Aviv University, Israel. The study observed individuals using their mobile phones in different locations on campus and included a survey of 138 students. The findings suggest that the public realm, as a social territory, is gradually being modified by individuals' use of technological devices.

In a somewhat similar vein, Lemish and Cohen (2005) examined the relationship between the mobile phone and identity in Israel. Key to their analysis is the examination of the different ways in which the mobile phone is enlisted in the "performance" of identity. Their findings show how Israelis construct various discourses around phone use in public—framing their identities in terms of gender, age and ethnicity (Lemish & Cohen, 2005).

Their findings suggest that the mobile phone in Israel has become an everyday, highly regarded, multipurpose interpersonal communication device rather than a working tool. Both men and women discussed their perceptions of the role of the mobile phone in their lives in quite a traditional gendered manner—activity and technological appropriation for men versus dependency and domesticity for women. At the same time, the actual phoning habits and attitudes of users point to a pattern of domestication of the mobile phone (Lemish & Cohen, 2005).

Similar to the findings from Israel, Fortunati (2000) suggests that public phone-talk can alter people's efforts at self-presentation, offering something of their backstage character while located on the publicly accountable front stage. She refers to the tension between self-presentation in the public physical space versus the personal space when talking on the phone.

Commonly, we give up our privacy in order to receive something in return.

ONE-WAY ROAD: THE 3G PRIVACY DEAL

On January 9, 2007 the term privacy was reborn. Apple entered the mobile phone market with the introduction of the iPhone. Possessing many of the abilities of an Internet-connected laptop computer, the iPhone quickly became one of the most popular and influential devices in the mobile phone market (Smith, 2010). People began to use their mobile phones for a wide variety of tasks, ranging from calling and texting to playing games, navigation, and social networking (Salehan & Negahban, 2013). With over 59 million iPhones sold in just a few months from its launch, iPhones seemed to be everywhere and Apple subsequently expanded their product line to include the iPod Touch and the iPad, both of which run the same software and share many of the same hardware features as the iPhone (Smith, 2010).

By 2011, there were over four billion mobile phone subscriptions worldwide (Christin et al., 2011). Apple has nearly 250,000 applications in its store and has served over three billion downloads. (Beresford, Rice & Skehin, 2011). Mobile phones expose users to different functional options such as GPS, virtual stores, cameras, social media, environmental sensors, physical monitoring and many other functions in addition to its initial purpose: to make a phone call. All of the above represent the reshaping of our culture, with mobile phone users being monitored and traced just by using a smartphone.

Nowadays, 3G technologies enable users to live through their smartphones. Social media has gained rapid popularity, providing users with several ways to connect to others using web, email and mobile applications (Salehan

& Negahban, 2013). For example, the Facebook mobile application is the most popular with over 650 million active users connected through mobile devices (Mashable, 2012). According to Lyons (2001), once the technology enabled users to access the social network sphere, for example, on mobile devices, a new practice of exposure was created. We may therefore conclude that voluntary privacy exposures, where people willingly reveal personal details about themselves, have become part of our interactive DNA.

In 2005, Jones and Soltren (2005) conducted a study on social media users' illusion of privacy. The findings revealed that 74% of social media users were aware of the Facebook's privacy options; yet only 62% actually used them. At the same time, over 70% of users willingly posted large amounts of personal information including demographic data, such as age, gender and location, demonstrating a disregard for both the privacy settings and Facebook's privacy policy.

Another study involving the complicated implications of smartphone use found that users continually negotiate and manage the tension between perceived privacy risks and expected benefits (Tufekci, 2008). It therefore becomes clear that our expectations of privacy have been reshaped in each generation of cellular technology, leading users to accept new levels of privacy loss.

Following the above, when exploring the continuous tension between smartphones and smartphone users, we can identify some kind of an unwritten agreement which involves the exposure of our identities in order to gain information about others. Ellison, Steinfield and Lampe (2007) showed that the most important benefit of online networks is probably the social capital resulting from creating and maintaining interpersonal relationships. Therefore, since the creation and preservation of this social capital is systematically built upon the voluntary disclosure of private information to a virtually unlimited audience. Consequently Ibrahim (2008) characterized this deal between users as complicit risk where personal information becomes social capital which is traded and exchanged.

Debatin, Lovejoy and Horn (2009) explain that social media users are found to exhibit higher risk-taking attitudes than individuals who are not members of the "online culture." Consequently, it can be assumed that the expected gratification motivates mobile users to provide and frequently update very specific personal (even intimate) data which most would immediately refuse to reveal in other contexts.

We can use Lauter and Wolfe's (1977) point of view to better understand the tension between the user and the smartphone in the battle for privacy. According to Lauter and Wolfe, while users express concern over how technological advances are "invading" their everyday lives and monitoring them constantly, they are also aware and active users, which leads the smartphone to its complete domination of the individual's perception of privacy. There-fore, we may conclude that users play a significant role in the reshaping of privacy boundaries in the online culture, mentioned above in Debatin, Lovejoy and Horn (2009).

APPLICATIONS AND PRIVACY: CAN THE TWO CO-EXIST?

Over the years, the popularity of mobile apps has continued to rise, as their usage has become increasingly prevalent among mobile phone users. Stud-ies reported that during the year 2012, more mobile subscribers used apps than browsed the Internet on their devices: 51.1% versus 49.8% respec-tively (Brown, 2014). In addition, mobile phone researchers found that mobile app usage strongly correlates with user context and depends on user location and time of the day ("Revolutionary apps," 2014). The numbers are remarkable—according to the Gartner market research firm, there were approximately 100 billion apps downloaded in 2013 (91% of them being non-fee) generating US $26 billion. Moreover, a number of different reports estimate that the app economy creates revenues of more than €10 billion per year within the European Union, while over 529,000 jobs have been created in 28 EU states due to the growth of the app market (Dredge, 2013).

In a digital society, where the conglomeration of different mobile apps generates a distinct interactive identify for each user, the growing amount of online personal content exposes users to a new set of privacy boundaries. Digital cameras, and lately a new technology of camera phone applications that can upload photos or video content directly to the web, make publishing personal content increasingly easy (Ahern et al., 2007). Therefore, multime-dia collections, which reveal much of users' personal and social environ-ments, are out in the public sphere and, by launching them, users expose rich aggregate information about themselves (Goggin, 2009). Apps and privacy collide not only in photos, but also in the endless life aspects shared by billions of users.

Over the years, a significant number of mobile applications have been released, invading another area of the personal sphere: enabling users to track each other. Some of these applications are driven by the desire of enterprises to increase the productivity of their employees. Others are geared toward supporting social networking scenarios, such as meeting up with friends, or safety-oriented scenarios, such as making sure that a loved one returns home safely (Sadeh et al., 2009). The growing number of mobile phones sold with location tracking technologies such as GPS, along with the emergence of Wi-Fi based location tracking solutions, led to mainstream adoption of these apps.

In their study, Sadeh et al. (2009) demonstrate that most users are not putting an effort into fully understanding how to articulate their privacy preferences. Their study examined use of the "People Finder" app that enables users to share their location with friends and family. The study found that users learn the privacy policies and terms over time, as they use the app. An additional example of the complicated relationship between apps and privacy appears in a study by Christin and colleagues (2011). They analyzed the many sensor-based applications in 2011 and examined the amount of personal information about users that could be inferred. The applications can collect sensory information by using mobile phone components such as camera, microphone, GPS receivers and Bluetooth. They found that without any suitable protection mechanism, mobile phones are transformed into miniature spies. Possible intrusions into a user's privacy include the recording of intimate discussions, taking photographs of private scenes or tracing a user's path and monitoring the locations he has visited.

For app users, privacy is guaranteed by the feeling of maintaining control over the release of their sensitive information (Christin et al., 2011). Yet sensor-based applications are able to collect the most intimate knowledge about the user's body, health, and location; one example is personal health monitoring applications. Mobile phones can be used to monitor the physiological state and health of users by employing embedded or external sensors. Privacy threats for such applications include the exposure of personal data such as private life, habits, acts and relationships.

When examining the coexistence of apps and privacy, it seems that the one cannot be separated from the other. Mobile adoption rates have skyrocketed with an estimated 1.75 billion smartphone subscribers worldwide in 2014 (Forbes, 2014). Naturally, as the numbers increase, the age of users tends to decrease as we have begun to see a large growth in the use of mobile phones apps, especially among youth using online social networking services. In their study, Salehan and Negahban (2013) showed that extensive use of technology could lead to addiction. Israeli teenagers are deeply involved in the interactive virtual sphere and spend an average of four hours per day on their mobile. The study found that the use of social networking mobile applications is a significant predictor of mobile addiction. The findings also demonstrate that the use of social networking applications is affected by both the social network size and the intensity of exposure that the user is committed to when using the app.

Social media apps are undoubtedly shaping and redefining the nature of communication among people all over the world. The border between the public and private sphere is being blurred and even our terminology has undergone a meaningful change. As Beresford and colleagues (2001) note, on

Facebook, users want to be "liked," on Twitter users hope to be "followed," on WhatsApp users are waiting to "be seen" and so on.

Marshall McLuhan (1967) famously predicted that technology would change us. However, did he predict that this kind of domination, led by smartphone use, would be accelerated by different applications? Whether McLuhan's statement is true can be deliberated, but the fact is that our personal DNA is comprised of small interactive pieces that can be accessed by anyone, anywhere (Salehan & Negahban, 2013). Along with widespread use of social networking apps on mobile phones, we are witnessing the disappearance of conventional privacy, which is being propelled by voluntary exposure of the users themselves.

APPLICATIONS AND PRIVACY: CASE STUDIES

Facebook Application: Created in 2012

The Facebook Mobile App was launched in 2012 with the goal of expanding the social media network's reach and increasing the number of users by leveraging different mobile devices and platforms. To those who have been following Facebook closely, the shift to mobiles was inevitable. More and more people are checking their Facebook messages on their mobile device and skipping the desktop version completely (Kabir & Auerbach, 2013). This is a behavioral shift in users that Facebook has both taken advantage of and perpetuated. Mark Zuckerberg, Facebook's founder, stated that in 2012, with the help of over a billion people, Facebook became a mobile company. The app has accounted for 23% of revenues, which in 2012 were over $1.59 billion (Olanoff, 2013).

When examined more thoroughly, the Facebook application is an interesting case of voluntary privacy exposure. The app allows physical, emotional and factual sharing: The user can enter pictures of himself and others (without their approval) as well as facts about their lives, for example, workplace, educational institution, place of residence, marital status, family relationships, and so on. The user can post a "status" of his private thoughts and his ideas to the members of his Facebook community, to all users in the public eye or just to his family or specific group of interest. In addition, the user can share other people's thoughts, articles, websites or other pages on the web. Moreover, the user can share his exact location at any given moment.

The application challenges private/personal boundaries through its exclusive features. For example, the feature "seen" indicates when a particular receiver has seen the message from a specific sender. Another application feature is the "active status," that indicates the specific time a user was active in the Facebook application. These features reflect our movement in virtual space and keep us constantly connected. Through use of the Facebook app, individual users take part in a predetermined accord in which user privacy boundaries are consistently being reshaped by voluntary privacy exposures.

In Israel, mobile app usage (specifically Facebook) is significant compared to other countries. More than 61% of all Israelis use the Facebook app on their mobile devices, with over 2.4 million entrances per day. Studies examining Israeli Facebook users found that attractive posts create higher involvement and exposure for users. This indicates the near obsession people have with daily use of the app. Therefore, Israel, which is known for high rates of mobile usage, has become a microcosm for the study of voluntary privacy exposure.

WhatsApp Application: Created in 2009

WhatsApp is a perfect example of how the privacy norms that were established in our culture have changed dramatically, especially from the user's point of view. The app is a cross-platform instant messaging service that enables users to share text messages, audio, images and their physical location with other users. In addition, it allows users to create groups and send messages to multiple members. It also enables users to set their own profile picture and create an entire interactive identity. Since its founding in 2009 by Brian Acton and Jan Koum, WhatsApp has become the most popular messaging app with over 600 million users. In 2014, WhatsApp was purchased by Facebook for $19 billion (Jackson, 2012).

WhatsApp's specific features as well as instantaneous service have reshaped our expectations concerning privacy. The apps "last seen" feature indicates the time and date a user was last seen using the app, while it's "typing or not" feature enables users to see when other users are online plus their physical status. If desired, one can choose to disable this feature so that other users will not be able to know when the user was last seen, but this means they will not be able to see the information regarding others (Wisniewski, 2013). This demonstrates how, in order to gain information, one must willingly give up one's own privacy. The instinct for gathering information is just more powerful than protecting our own privacy nowadays.

With over 72 billion messages being sent each day, we can confidently say that WhatsApp has led to the rapid transfer of information (Tzuk, 2013). In Israel, the adoption rate of the app to smartphones is 92%, which has made WhatsApp one of the most popular apps in the country. A special survey conducted in 2013 by Millward Brown Institute in Israel, showed that, on average, Israelis spend 3 hours a day using WhatsApp to send visual and textual information to one another (Liel, 2014).

However, WhatsApp's instant transfer ability also enables offensive or privacy information about others (without their consent) to go viral. In Israel there have been a few incidents where users had personal information about themselves, like videos and photos, shared with others without their consent. For example, a young Israeli girl ("Y") had an intimate video taken of her by her former partner. Although she thought the video would be sent to her phone only via the app, the former partner sent the video to his friends, who transferred it to other users. In two weeks, the chain of transfer led to almost a million users having received the video on their cellphones. Y's life was ruined and since then she has been hospitalized and placed under psychological care ("The intimate affair," 2013).

Y's story is only one example of hundreds of situations in which users operated in a sort of "privacy illusion." While users know the risks involved in documenting personal information through apps, they continue to willingly expose themselves.

The latest example of increased privacy exposure through WhatsApp is the blue check mark feature which indicates whether a message has been read. At the beginning WhatsApp used a green mark that notified users whether or not a message had been delivered and received by the recipient's phone ("Frequently asked questions," 2015). Now users can fully monitor whether their message has been read. This is certainly an example of the escalation of the ongoing breaches of our privacy boundaries. However, users enjoy the privilege of monitoring others and therefore the privacy invasion seems minor.

SECRET Application: Created in 2014

The Secret application enables anonymous emotional and factual sharing: It is an anonymous alternative to Facebook. The application imports the user's Facebook members who use the app as well, but leaves all users of the application and its members anonymous, with no identity, no names and no pictures. The anonymity allows users to post thoughts, opinions, gossip, criticism and reviews anonymously to their friends and acquaintances from Facebook without paying the social cost. Publishing gossip, exposing intimate confessions, publishing lies, accusations, embarrassing truths and secrets of others can be devastating on Facebook, and Secret is the perfect arena for it.

Nine months from the app inauguration in San Francisco, Secret has raised $25 million from a group of investors, making it one of the only start-ups to reach such levels of funding so quickly (Lunden, 2014). At present, the app has reached a value of $100 million as one of the highest ranks in the app interactive stores (Macmillan, 2014). In 2014 the app received an "official stamp" as a complicated case regarding privacy issues. A Brazilian court granted a preliminary injunction to a public prosecutor that prohibits Apple, Google, and Microsoft from distributing the app and also compels the three companies to remotely delete the app on users' devices in the country (Geuss, 2014). The prosecutor sought the injunction after receiving user complaints of anonymous bullying and life-threats from users.

Secret represents a dramatic increase in the range of voluntary privacy exposure. By using the app, users actively agree to a "deal" that includes risking their own privacy and becoming potential victims of social shaming. The app has the most significant influence upon social networks users. Just in Israel, there have been thousands of reports to the official computer crimes police department against users who exposed private information about others (Aini, 2014). Some Secret users claim to have been mentally and emotional injured due to extremely private information about them being posted without their consent. This includes videos and photos taken of them which reveal sexual abuse, without their approval or awareness of the presence of a camera.

SKYPE Application: Created in 2003

The Skype application enables physical, emotional and factual sharing: It can be used to audio or video call people all over the world. Skype video calls enable users to reveal their faces, bodies, and voices to other users. Skype also offers conference calls with other users all over the world and makes it possible to share video files, pictures, documents, screen shots and text messages with other users. Skype's benefits, beyond the free and low-cost calls, are said to include easy set up and good audio and visual quality. While logged in, users can see which of their contacts is also online and be alerted when new people log in.

According to a 2012 Skype report, there are 47 million users in the US and 300 million worldwide. The typical Skype user is young and socially engaged. The audience is almost evenly split between male and female (52% male, 48% female) and more than half are between the ages of 18–35 (Williams et al., 2014). In 2011, Microsoft bought Skype for 8.5 billion dollars (Wauters, 2011).

The Skype mobile app enables simple video and voice calls from one's mobile phone. It is often used for business calls as well as providing a way for romantic couples to stay connected. Due to its simple calling and mobile features, it is very common to see individuals using Skype in public spaces, such as coffee shops or shopping centers, and thus transferring and sharing private information across the screen.

NOKNOK Application: Created in 2003

The Noknok application has become enormously popular due, in part, to its facilitation of easy fact sharing. In the first few months in Israel, Noknok reached over 57,000 downloads and the numbers kept rising (Kvir, 2014). Noknok enables users to see all the names by which other users have listed them in their mobile phones, such as: "Joe, do not answer," "the ugly girl from the bar," but the application does not reveal the name-caller's identity, just the name used to call the user. The application also enables users to identify unknown numbers and collect information about callers through social networks. For example, the app enables a user to identify who is calling him/her by showing a live ID (name & picture) of the caller, even if he is not in the user's contact list.

Noknok obtains most of its information from users' contacts and social networks. However, it also collects information on users who have not provided their consent and/or have not download the application. This means that even if a specific user did not download the app himself—he is probably already in the database because one of his friends download it, or because he uses social networks.

Noknok is an interesting case of voluntary privacy exposure. The user agrees to reveal his identity to the app, and, in return, is able to identify everyone who calls him. Users "take back control" (the ability to identify unknown callers) while, at the same time, take a social risk by agreeing to the exposure of their names (and how they are referred to) on other peoples' phones.

While Noknok's founders claim to put privacy first (Yaron, 2014), the amount of data the app collects tells a different story. Nevertheless, judging by users' behavior and willingness to use the app, it seems that users are willing to forget all about their privacy terms, because this is part of the deal with the Noknok app.

TINDER Application: Created in 2012

TINDER is a dating/hook-up app that allows physical, emotional and factual sharing. The app connects to the user's Facebook profile, draws a number of random profile photos and limited personal data such as the user's interests, hometown and first name. It then displays his/her picture and first name to other users close to his hometown (by GPS). The app's gimmick is that two users can connect successfully only if the two of them have "liked" each other. Justin Matin, chief marketing officer of Tinder and its co founder, told a Calcalist newspaper reporter that Tinder produces more than two million connections each day (Harari, 2013). The average user enters Tinder 11 times a day, each time for nearly seven minutes, amounting to 77 minutes a day.

In Israel, usage grew at 4% to 5% per day, and 1% of the population uses Tinder (Harari, 2013). It is an amazing rate of use, especially in Israeli app phone culture, which has developed rapidly.

In the dating world in general and in Israel in particular, Tinder has become a dating game-changer for users in their twenties. The entire Tinder experience is designed to be familiar and emulate the way we interact in real life—digitally reproduced, enhanced, and made mobile. The app's significant popularity in Israel is due to its authentic character. You "like" people in the same way you would "like" them in a bar or on other platforms for face-to-face interaction—where you find them attractive at first glance.

At first sight, Tinder app seems to maintain some anonymity, as all users are presented only by their first names with none of their details being accessible to strangers. However, it takes only a little effort to find an "anonymous" user's complete profile. By simply matching some of the details from the partner's profile, one can find the complete name, mutual friends, romantic background and other information. Therefore, in contrast to prior versions of dating apps, where details were exposed once both sides were able to trust one another, Tinder users agree to give up another crucial layer of the conventional privacy demands: They actively participate in the dissemination of their personal status, their sexual preferences, their romantic desires and ideals.

INSTAGRAM Application: Created in 2010

Instagram is a photo and video sharing application which allows physical and factual sharing. It enables users to edit and share photos taken using a mobile device. Users can also tag other users in photos, share photo locations and provide a personal caption for their photos.

The name Instagram is derived from the word "instant," a quick snapshot that can be seen immediately, and "telegram," a message sent to friends all over the world. The founders declare that photos are public by default and are visible to anyone using Instagram or on the instagram.com website. If the user chooses to make his account private, only people who follow him on the Instagram application will be able to see his/her photos.

In a 2013 survey polling 7,200 teenagers across 41 states in the US, Instagram was voted the favorite social media network on smart phones (Thompson, 2014). In terms of social media, Instagram is the highest preferred marketing channel at 38% compared to Twitter at 34% and Facebook at 21%. In 2012, Facebook acquired Instagram for $1 billion. Instagram hit 30 million iOS users in only 18 months and was downloaded millions of times within 24 hours when launched on Android (Chowdhry, 2014).

Instagram is breaking all concepts of conventional privacy. Many users opt to keep their photos public and accessible to anyone because they want to attract followers—other users who admire and look at their photos. Thus, "followers" are people who voluntarily give up their privacy in order to follow others. It is a trade privacy deal—where one exposes his "backyard" to all Instagram users, including exact location and personal details—in exchange for following others.

When analyzing the cultural implications of Instagram in general and in Israeli society in particular, we can discern, for example, an increase in the term "selfie"—a self-portrait photograph, typically taken with a hand held digital camera or camera phone. The trend of taking a "selfie" using Instagram may help us understand the voluntary exposure of privacy which occurs almost automatically among users. A global trend which began on Instagram was the "post-orgasm selfie" in which users uploaded self-photos of themselves with their spouse in a variety of vaguely sexual moments. In general, the popularity of selfies on Instagram has been astounding. Over 53 million photos tagged with the hashtag #selfie and the word "selfie" were mentioned in Instagram status updates over 368,000 times during a one-week period in October 2013.

Snapchat **Application: Created in 2012**

The Snapchat app is an interesting example of privacy illusion. Users can send photos to one another via chat, but the image is deleted immediately from the chat box within 10 seconds. This way, users feel comfortable sending intimate pictures or images since they know these will quickly be deleted (and are thus unable to be "shared"). According to the app data collected in 2014, users were sending 700 million photos and videos per day, while Snapchat Stories content was being viewed 500 million times per day. By October 2014, the company was valued at $10 billion (Jain, 2014).

While Snapchat bases its whole product marketing on the auto-deletion of the snaps (images and videos) so that they are not stored, recent reports indicate otherwise. In 2014 hackers gained access to approximately 90,000 pictures and 9,000 videos sent over Snapchat. These snaps were most likely captured by some third-party app whose database was compromised of these hackers. Due to this invasion, users realized that the snaps are stored in company servers for at least 30 days, even if they are not viewed (Stern, 2014).

WAZE **Application: Created in 2008**

The popularity of the Waze application symbolizes an interesting case of the erosion of privacy boundaries. By using Waze, users voluntarily reveal a significant amount of information about themselves to a whole slew of parties. Even so, Waze represents the perfect balance between continuously updated map information and consistent social needs in the on line media culture. Due to the option of factual sharing, users can produce the world's first real-time map by drivers all over the world. It is not only a navigation service but also a social mobile application that enables drivers to alert one another to traffic and accidents, weather reports and other crucial information to drivers, and most important—chat with each other during the ride. The latest version of Waze enables users to import their mobile contact list to the app.

The Israeli app accurately addressed users' needs by adding a social platform to navigational capabilities. In addition to being able to talk (chat) with one another, the app incorporates gamification features in which users are awarded points for allowing the app to track their commute, or for manually entering travel information, all of which can be viewed by other users. These features further blur private/public boundaries as users automatically become part of the information chain that constructs the app. Waze even partnered with the Federal Emergency Management Agency (FEMA) and Google in the days after Hurricane Sandy which hit America in 2012, to help identify gas stations that had run out of gas. Waze also partners with other commercial organizations, as the app tracks a user's location in order to provide geo-based advertising content (Couts, 2013).

Waze has managed to establish itself as an absolute necessity for drivers around the world. As of January 2012, the app had been downloaded 12 million times worldwide. In July 2012 Waze announced that it had reached 20 million users, half of them recruited in a period of only six months and by June 2013 there were nearly 50 million Waze users around the world (Federman & Rosenthal, 2013).

Waze was developed by the creative hands of Israelis. Israel, a 67-year-old independent country, which more than six decades ago had no natural resources and a limited water supply and whose land mass consisted largely of desert, is solely depended on the natural creativity of its people. This creativity has flourished in the technological realm as illustrated by Waze, among others. Many Israeli technological innovations and developments have enriched lives across the planet. Waze is only one of the successful start-ups that have made Israel the country with the largest number of start-ups per capita in the world and a leading player in the world of high-tech innovations.

Grindr Application: Created in 2008

One of the well-known apps which has reconstructed the conventional privacy norms is Grindr. It is a geo-social networking application geared toward gay, bisexual, and bi-curious men, which has built its reputation around the idea of discretion. This enables "in the closet" users, some of whom are singles and some involved in relationships with women, to use the app in order to explore their sexuality.

The registering process requires a list of data—verified picture (not necessarily a face picture), e-mail address, permission to be monitored by location and so on. The district monitor goes against the inherent logic of privacy and gives away the user's identity. The app makes use of the device's geolocation, which allows users to locate other men within close proximity. The technique is accomplished through a user interface that displays a grid of men's pictures, arranged from nearest to farthest away. Tapping on a picture will display a brief profile for that user, as well as the option to chat, send pictures, and share one's location (Kincaid, 2009).

Grinder has become the largest and most popular gay mobile app. Building a significant global community, the app has become available in 192 countries around the world (Lewallen, 2014) and has been recognized as a huge success in Israel with over 100,000 downloads to cell phones over the last two years (Watts, 2011). In the Israeli view of gay dating apps, Grindr replaced the app "Atraf," which was previously on the top of the chart for gay people and supplied a platform for romantic and sexual introductions.

Grindr symbolizes an interesting example of privacy control negotiating. While privacy boundaries are challenged frequently by GPS-based geosocial apps, it is of the utmost importance on gay networks. Without proper security measures, haters and bigots could easily download such an app and use it to pinpoint targets for potentially violent encounters. In 2014 Egyptians admitted that spies were using the Grindr dating app to catch gays in the act and arrest them for what is illegal activity in their country (Culzac, 2014).

Another case in which the voluntary exposure of users led to a public shaming occurred in Berlin, Germany. Dries Verhoeven, an artist, streamed conversations with a man who was chatting with him on Grindr, onto the side of a building in a busy public square in the city. This outrageous act humiliated the man who was on his way to meet his interlocutor at their set location. Once he spotted their conversation screened for the public to see, he immediately pressed charges against the artist who had exposed him as an "artistic cause" (McCormick, 2014). Clearly, Grindr and other dating apps, surround their users with the illusion of privacy, but one that that is warped and contributes to privacy distortion.

LOSING MY PRIVACY: ANALYZING CASE STUDIES OF SMARTPHONE USE

In order to analyze the level and character of public exposure via mobile phones, our research assistants conducted a participant observation and collected 40 case studies—examples of individuals sharing private information in the public sphere between January and September 2014 based on the typology presented in the previous chapters.

We found that the level of factual, emotional and physical exposure is extremely high while using mobile phones in public spaces; it seems that individuals are just slightly aware or not aware at all of how they are sharing intimate details in public. Surprisingly, we found that people talk loudly about private subjects in public, knowing that they are not in a private sphere. Subjects included infidelity, infertility, career problems, relationship problems and family difficulties.

We collected data on the wide range of mobile phone uses of people in public spaces. These included telephone calls, Skype calls, face-time conversations, uploading of pictures to Instagram or Facebook, GPS, WhatsApp and more. Our case studies took place in public spaces such as trains, busses, malls, stores, banks, pools, cafés, restaurants and streets.

Our observations revealed that situations in which individuals conducted private conversations in public often made involuntarily listeners feel uncomfortable, disturbed and even hostile vis-à-vis these conversations by strangers. These situations also do harm to the speaker's privacy, the privacy of the person on the other end of the line and the privacy of the people who are mentioned in the conversation.

We ranked the level of privacy exposure from 1 to 4 according to our privacy typology. The following cases (see below) are examples of individuals sharing private factual and visual information with strangers. When talking about medical information, people revealed the results of medical tests, diseases or talked about relatives who were having fertility problems. When talking about financial information, people discussed financial assets such as stocks, debts to banks, future inheritance and they provided credit card details. People also reported on their locations via mobile phones, sharing the name/location of specific places as well as using GPS apps and Facebook to identify their location.

However, the most common type of disclosure involved people exposing their relationships, sometimes complicated, with their immediate personal environment: friends, family and spouses as well as parent-child and parent-teacher relationships. Relationship issues were revealed publicly through the sharing of stories, involving personal information about the speaker and others, information which is often considered private.

Parent and Child Conversations

A woman in her 20's was riding the train and in the presence of other passengers, was speaking on her mobile phone about her father's infidelity to her mother. From the conversation, one could understand that the woman was speaking to her mother and that the mother had caught the father in an illicit relationship and had been to his lover's house to confront him. During the conversation the daughter repeatedly responded saying, "Mom, don't believe him, don't be naïve . . . ," "No way she's just a colleague," "It isn't the first time . . ." "He lost me a long time ago, I have nothing to tell him," and other harsh responses.

This is an example of the type of call in which speakers are completely absorbed in the conversation and unaware of their immediate environment. Moreover, since the conversation took place in a crowded train, with few places to "escape" to, the other passengers were forced to listen to it. The conversation exposes factual information that harms the speaker's privacy and that of her mother and father, as well as the passengers' right not to hear the disturbing call.

The next case involves a man sharing intimate physical and factual information about his daughter. A man in his 50's was sitting in line at the bank and swiping through pictures of his granddaughter's fetal ultrasound on his phone. When he realized that he was being watched by the man sitting next to him, the older man excitedly turned to the man and shared the photos with him—even though they were very intimate and revealing pictures of his daughter's womb. The older man even initiated a conversation with the other man, stating, "I'm amazed that today you can watch your unborn granddaughter on your phone." The conversation raises questions about whether or not he was aware of his daughter's privacy concerns when he shared her photos with a stranger. This case is also an example of how intimate visual and factual information sharing with strangers becomes legitimate everyday content.

The third case is another example of how unaware individuals are of speaking about private matters in a public environment. A man was sitting with his 9-year-old son in a waiting room, talking on his mobile phone about his ex-wife (the mother of the boy) with whom he had had a heated argument. He used harsh words to describe the mother, even accusing her of criminal fraud. The boy listened in silence to his father and looked embarrassed. Other people sitting in the waiting room reacted to the father's call and gave him advice—the debate about the "crazy ex-wife" became the waiting room "talk of the day." This case shows that sharing private calls in a public space can create a "support group" that allows the speaker to tell, distribute, receive advice and reassurance from the environment around him.

Parent and Teacher Conversations

Mobile phone conversations between parents and teachers were mainly about students' misconduct. There were cases in which the speaker revealed personal information about the child, the child's family or the child's teachers. One of the most revealing conversations between a mother and her child's teacher occurred on the train: "Look, the child comes from a difficult home; my husband isn't easy with our children," the mother told the teacher apologetically, and began describing a violent father. When it seemed that the teacher was trying to explain that violence is not the way to educate children, the mother responded, "I know that violence is not a solution, but if your child spat on you and cursed you, wouldn't you slap him?"

The mother, who speaks openly in the public sphere about domestic violence, is exposing herself and her family to the possibility that someone from the relevant authorities (such as police or child welfare office) may listen to the call and report her. The mother is publicly admitting that her husband is violent—an example of how an issue being discussed, that would have formerly been considered taboo in public, is being shared with strangers in a public space, even if the mother's loud conversation about domestic violence means that she is unaware of her surroundings. It appears that many subjects that were once considered shameful and embarrassing, are now considered legitimate subjects of public conversation on mobile phones or Facebook.

Romantic Partners' Conversations

Intimate conversations including longing expressions of love are heard loud and clear in the public sphere. Intimate fights between lovers and even screams or complaints of infidelity, secrets and lies take place. We can also see how couples share emotional and visual expressions of their relationships on mobile apps.

In one of our case studies, we noticed a young man in his 20's walking down the street while talking with his girlfriend on Skype. The two were engaged in a sexy conversation on the street using "bedroom language."

Even the bedroom, one of the most private and intimate spaces in people's homes, has become a public place when using a mobile phone: in one of our case studies, a young woman posted photos of herself with her boyfriend in bed on her Facebook page, captioned: "I'm sure I'll have a good night, and you?" Others replied with comments like: "Why are you sharing this with us?" "Too much information," and other criticisms. The girl answered: "If I'm going to fuck with my boyfriend, that's my business." Indeed, this is a clear example of the blurring of the spaces and of physical and emotional exposure. After she had shared her bedroom activity, she then decided that no one had the right to criticize her actions on Facebook.

Conversations with Friends

In another case study, we spotted a group of teenagers sitting together in a cafe scanning through revealing pictures of other teenagers while making sarcastic comments as they passed the phone from one to another and laughed about the pictured teenagers' bodies and positions. We also observed a woman taking "selfie" pictures in a clothing store dressing room, half-dressed, while changing outfits and uploading them to Facebook.

Shame associated with the naked body slowly disappears as public exposure of body parts become increasingly popular. It is not unusual to upload revealing photos to Instagram and Facebook, or to send them using WhatsApp. The fact is that people take pictures of themselves and others all the time, even in places which were considered private in the past; they then upload the photos to the social network, clearly a public space, and wait for "likes" and comments from others. This is a further example of the growing blurriness between the public and the private sphere.

CONCLUSION

You Exist if You're "Liked"

This chapter shows that mobile communication is a technology that marks the end of privacy. The mobile almost becomes part of our bodies; most people in the developed world are unable to leave home without their phones, or to put them down for more than a few hours, without been disturbed by their absence. We are close to the day when phones will be attached to our bodies, similar to glasses and a watch, and may perhaps take the form of a computer implanted under the skin. The technology is here, as is our desire to conjoin with it. Smartphones are at the same time a complete expression of our personal and private world, and a device that eliminates the ability to isolate the public from the personal.

In our smartphones we store and express our personal world: our friends, personal documents, photos, links, favorite sites, conversations and all the sensitive information about us, including bank account details, medical tests, and intimate moments. All of this information is allegedly protected by passwords, available exclusively to us, but in fact, it is within the reach of the world that surrounds us, and is actually very easily revealed to strangers.

The smartphone is usually with us in the public sphere, and we use it whether we are in the company of friends or strangers or alone in our homes. The screen is visible not only for us but for everyone around us. As we have seen in our small anthropological research, through simple observations we encountered a variety of mobile uses that have one thing in common: While using mobile phones, people often forget that they are surrounded by strangers. In other cases, they simply forget the device or lose it, or pass it on to others with all of their private information exposed on it. For example, an

Israeli high school teacher left her tablet in class, and the students found her nude photos on it. The photos were taken privately on her phone and she did not know that her mobile phone was synchronized with her tablet (Seidler & Scope, 2014).

But the heart of the matter is not only that. The mobile is used to fill much more profound needs: the need to be connected at all times, the need to be "LIKED" and the need to be seen. These needs involve a great loss of privacy, even without noting the sacrifice we make. Today, more than ever, there is the feeling that unless you document your activities and upload them to the virtual world, they have not really happened. The event is more meaningful if it is documented at all times and especially if it is uploaded to the virtual space where it can gain the reactions and comments of others— especially the "likes."

A very interesting case we found that highlights the phenomenon mentioned above involved a woman in her mid-20's who uploaded a series of photos to Facebook documenting her marriage proposal. The first image was a photo of her partner kneeling and asking her to marry him. She then labeled the place where the proposal took place and uploaded another image of a romantic dinner with candlelight and flowers on the table. Another photo featured the engagement ring on her finger. A few minutes later she uploaded a picture of her boyfriend kissing her with the caption, "Yeah, engaged to the love of my life." Finally she changed her relationship status on Facebook from "in a relationship" to "engaged." You can only imagine the situation as the woman stopped the flow of events in order to document them. Did she ask her boyfriend to stay kneeling for the picture? Did she let him first say the words and only then take the photo? Instead of responding with joy and a hug, did she first freeze for the photo and then react? These questions point out how one of the most emotional and significant events in a couple's life, the marriage proposal, has become a social and even a virtual event.

Besides documenting wedding proposals, we have encountered an additional series of cellular photo-trends. These include the intimate moments people have captured pertaining to their private lives. On February 2015, a new phenomenon hit the social media when women all over the world started taking "brelfies"—a selfie picture while breast-feeding their infant in all types of intimate positions (Waterlow, 2015). Originally, the purpose was to call for legitimization of breast-feeding in public. Seemingly, this political rationale encouraged women to join the trend. After thousands of women started posting images of themselves and their breastfed babies online, negotiating their privacy for an ideological fight inevitably led to questions of how/why this motivation had developed. Was the drive for political change the reason for the tide of "brelfies" posted online? Or was this perhaps a trend that started as an ideological battle, but soon became another excuse for people to voluntary expose themselves and to be shown and seen on various social networks? One way or another, the "brelfie," like other phone-trends, has contributed to the blur between private and public and changed our perceptions of the idea of online exposure.

In this chapter we have conducted a broad review in order to show the variety of uses and applications designed to facilitate the creation of a relationship between people in a variety of fields. By the time this book is published, we believe many new applications will emerge, yet their essence is the same: they offer us more knowledge about others, more sharing of information with those around us, more opportunities to show ourselves, to get feedback, and in a word—to share.

True, a vague illusion exists that users are in control of the information that flows from them and the information that they consume, but this illusion is no more than a mental mechanism of protection and denial. It is now clear to everyone that the "Big Brother" is much stronger. The media openly engage in a discourse of concern, fear and terror: the government is following us, giant corporations know everything about us, Google brings up every reference mentioning us, but in fact, the public does not really care. We continue to use these tracking devices, attach them to us, and freely report what we are doing.

Personally, most of us still want to control personal information, and talk about privacy as an important value, but as a society, we act decisively and continuously in the opposite direction. Most of us do not change the privacy settings of the various applications; we do not give up the download of useful tools, just because they involve the collection of personal information about us.

The smartphone is a technology that allows mobile exposure in all of its dimensions. first of all, factual information, which we distribute all the time, in almost every use of the mobile app; second, physical exposure: widespread use of the camera, self-timer, "selfies," including in many cases photographs in swimwear, lingerie and in the nude; thirdly, emotional exposure through numerous applications in real time allows us to express a range of feelings from anger, rage, and frustration to love, happiness and satisfaction.

The proximity and social connections that are created using a mobile phone give the illusion of intimacy and familiarity with others. We are indeed in touch with many, but these relationships can interfere with actual physical connections in real life. WhatsApp, Instagram and Facebook penetrate and integrate with the physical reality of the present time and place. We are not alone, but not really with those closest to us.

The progress of technology and mobile applications is very fast, but also involves temporary withdrawals. As mentioned in the application review, WhatsApp recently launched a new feature that allows using two blue V signs, to know whether the other party of the conversation not only received the message, but also read it. After a short period, due to protests, WhatsApp retracted and allowed users to opt out of this new feature. Soon we will probably forget this problem with WhatsApp; we will probably become accustomed to new uses, new surveillance, and the elimination of the boundaries that were once so clear.

Soon enough, mobile phone usage will approach a climax because of our aspiration to NOT be alone. We carry friends, contacts, social networking partners, as well as the history and information of our lives and of the world in our pockets wherever we go. We are part of something bigger; we can get anywhere immediately. We can find answers to every question; we are able to see and be seen. As time goes by, mobile phones will become an increasing part of us, a part of our bodies, and a direct connection to the world, eliminating the boundaries between the private and the public.

REFERENCES

(2013 January 15). The intimate affair that was exposed on the net. *Night Pipeline*. Retrieved from http://net.nana10.co.il/Article/?ArticleID=951400.

(2015). WhatsApp frequently asked questions. *WhatsApp*. Retrieved from https://www.whatsapp.com/faq/en/android/28000015.

Ahern, S., Eckles, D., Good, N.S., King, S., Naaman, M., & Nair, R. (2007). Overexposed? Privacy patterns and considerations in online and mobile photo sharing. In *Proceedings of the SIGCHI Conference on Human Factors in Computing Systems* (pp. 357–366). *ACM*.

Aini, R.H. (2014). Petah Tikva: Complaints of violations of the secret app. *Ynet Online*. Retrieved from http://www.mynet.co.il/articles/0,7340,L-4576461,00.html.

Almog, O. (2000). *The Sabra: The creation of the new Jew*. Univ of California Press, 1–20.

Beresford, A.R., Rice, A., Skehin, N., & Sohan, R. (2011). MockDroid: Trading privacy for application functionality on smartphones. In *Proceedings of the 12th Workshop on Mobile Computing Systems and Applications* (pp. 49–54). ACM.

Böhmer, M., Hecht, B., Schöning, J., Krüger, A., & Bauer, G. (2011). Falling asleep with Angry Birds, Facebook and Kindle: A large scale study on mobile application usage. In *Proceedings of the 13th International Conference on Human Computer Interaction with Mobile Devices and Services* (pp. 47–56). ACM.

Brown, M. (2014, May 27). 5 pitfalls mobile app developers face when it comes to HIPAA compliance. *TrueVault*. Retrieved from https://www.truevault.com/blog/5-pitfalls-mobile-app-developers-face-when-it-comes-to-hipaa-compliance.html#.VHRlFouUeCo

Christin, D., Reinhardt, A., Kanhere, S.S., & Hollick, M. (2011). A survey on privacy in mobile participatory sensing applications. *Journal of Systems and Software*, *84*(11), 1928–1946.

Chowdhry, A. (2014, October 13). Survey says teenagers prefer Instagram over Facebook. *Forbes*. Retrieved from http://www.forbes.com/sites/amitchowdhry/2014/10/13/survey-says-teenagers-prefer-instagram-over-facebook/.

Couts, A. (2013, March 3). Terms & conditions. Waze is a privacy accident waiting to happen. *Digital Trends*. http://www.digitaltrends.com/mobile/terms-conditions-waze-privacy-accident/.

Cui, Y., Chipchase, J., & Ichikawa, F. (2007). A cross culture study on phone carrying and physical personalization. In *Usability and Internationalization. HCI and Culture* (pp. 483–492). Berlin Heidelberg: Springer.

Culzac, N. (2014, September 17). Egypt's police 'using social media and ppls like Grindr to trap gay people.' *Independent*. Retrieved from http://www.independent.co.uk/news/world/africa/egypts-police-using-social-media-and-apps-like-grindr-to-trap-gay-people-9738515.html.

Debatin, B., Lovejoy, J.P., Horn, A.K., & Hughes, B.N. (2009). Facebook and online privacy: Attitudes, behaviors, and unintended consequences. *Journal of Computer-Mediated Communication, 15*(1), 83–108.

Dredge, S. (2013, September 19). Mobile app revenues tipped to reach $26bn in 2013. *The Guardian*. Retrieved from http://www.theguardian.com/technology/appsblog/2013/sep/19/gartner-mobile-apps-revenues-report.

Ellison, N.B., Steinfield, C., & Lampe, C. (2007). The benefits of Facebook "friends:" Social capital and college students' use of online social network sites. *Journal of Computer-Mediated Communication, 12*(4), 1143–1168.

Falaki, H., Mahajan, R., Kandula, S., Lymberopoulos, D., Govindan, R., & Estrin, D. (2010). Diversity in smartphone usage. In *Proceedings of the 8th International Conference on Mobile Systems, Applications, and Services* (pp. 179–194). ACM.

Federman, J., & Rosenthal, M.J. (2013 June 12). Waze sale signals new growth for Israeli high tech. *Yahoo News*. Retrieved from https://news.yahoo.com/waze-sale-signals-growth-israeli-high-tech-174533585.html.

Forbes (31, December 2014). Google in 2014. *Forbes Online*. Retrieved from: http://www.forbes.com/sites/greatspeculations/2014/12/31/google-in-2014/.

Fortunati, L. (2000). The mobile phone: New social categories and relations. *Information, Communication and Society*, 4, 513–528.

Geuss, M. (2014, August 20). Brazil court to Apple, Google: Wipe anonymous sharing app off users' phone. *ArsTechnica*. Retrieved from http://arstechnica.com/tech-policy/2014/08/brazil-court-to-apple-google-wipe-anonymous-sharing-app-off-users-phones/.

Goggin, G. (2006). *Cell phone culture: Mobile technology in everyday life*. United Kingdom: Routledge.

Hatuka, T., & Toch, E. (2014). The emergence of portable private-personal territory: Smartphones, social conduct and public spaces. *Urban Studies*.

Harari, K.T. (2013 September 24). Who said 'awake' and didn't receive. *Calcalist*. [Hebrew]. Retrieved from http://www.calcalist.co.il/articles/0,7340,L-3612745,00.html.

Harb, Z. (2011). Arab revolutions and the social media effect. *M/C Journal, 14*(2).

Ibrahim, Y. (2008). The new risk communities: Social networking sites and risk. *International Journal of Media & Cultural Politics, 4*(2), 245–253.

Jackson, E. (2012, March 12). Why selling WhatsApp to Facebook would be the biggest mistake of Jan Koum's and Brian Acton's lives. *Forbes.* Retrieved from http://www.forbes.com/sites/ericjackson/2012/12/03/why-selling-whatsapp-to-facebook-would-be-the-biggest-mistake-of-jan-koums-and-brian-actons-lives/.

Jain, N. (2014, October 16). The snappening; who to blame? *Tequs.* Retrieved from http://tequs.com/the-snappening-who-to-blame/.

Jones, H., & Soltren, J.H. (2005). Facebook: Threats to privacy. *Project MAC: MIT Project on Mathematics and Computing, 1.*

Kabir, O., & Auerbach, M. (2013, May 21). Facebook reveals: How many Israeli social network users. *The Calcalist.* [Hebrew] Retrieved from http://www.calcalist.co.il/internet/articles/0,7340,L-3602989,00.html

Katz, J.E., & Aakhus, M. (Eds.). (2002). *Perpetual contact: Mobile communication, private talk, public performance.* Cambridge: Cambridge University Press.

Kimmerling, B., & Moore, D. (1997). Collective identity as agency and structuration of society: The Israeli example 1. *International Review of Sociology, 7*(1), 25–49.

Kincaid, J. (2009, March 25). Gay dating making its way to the iPhone. *TechCrunch.* Retrieved from http://techcrunch.com/2009/03/25/gay-dating-makes-its-way-to-the-iphone/

Kvir, O. (2014, August 20). NokNok application: New Israeli hit has a dubious past. *Calcalist.* [Hebrew]. Retrieved from http://www.calcalist.co.il/internet/articles/0,7340,L-3638838,00.html.

Laufer, R.S., & Wolfe, M. (1977). Privacy as a concept and a social issue: A multidimensional developmental theory. *Journal of Social Issues, 33*(3), 22–42.

Lemish, D., & Cohen, A.A. (2005). Tell me about your mobile and I'll tell you who you are: Israelis talk about themselves. In R. Ling and P. Pedersen (Eds.), *Mobile communications* (pp. 187–202). London: Springer.

Lemish, D., & Cohen, A.A. (2005). On the gendered nature of mobile phone culture in Israel. *Sex Roles, 52*(7–8), 511–521.

Lewallen, S. (2014, April 1). The co-founder behind gay social app Grindr opens up about success, sanity and happiness. *Entrepreneur Online.* Retrieved from http://www.entrepreneur.com/article/232672.

Liel, D. (2014, February 5). What really happens on children's WhatsApp? *Mako Online News.* [Hebrew]. Retrieved from http://www.mako.co.il/news-israel/education/Article-5420cb160c30441004.htm.

Lunden, I. (2014, July 14). Anonymish app secret has raised another $25M, adds Facebook login and collections. *TechCrunch.* Retrieved from http://techcrunch.com/2014/07/14/anonymish-app-secret-has-raised-another-25m-adds-facebook-login-and-collections/.

Lyon, D. (2001). *Surveillance society: Monitoring everyday life.* McGraw-Hill International.

Macmillan, D. (2014, July 14). Secret's valuation hits $100 million in just nine months. *The Wallstreet Journal Blog.* Retrieved from http://blogs.wsj.com/digits/2014/07/14/secrets-valuation-hits-100-million-in-just-nine-months/.

McLuhan, M., & Fiore, Q. (1967). *The medium is the message,* (pp. 126–128). New York: Bantam.

McCormick, J.P. (2014, October 6). Artist who publicly projected Grindr chats ends exhibition after complaints and protest. *Pink News.* Retrieved from https://www. pinknews.co.uk/2014/10/06/artist-who-publicly-projected-grindr-chats-ends-exhibition-after-complaints/

Olanoff, D. (2013, January 30). For the first time, Facebook's 680M mobile MAUs surpassed desktop daus—Zuck says it's now a 'mobile company.' *TechCrunch.* Retrieved from http://techcrunch.com/2013/01/30/for-the-first-time-facebook-mobile-daus-exceeded-web-daus-in-q4–2012/Revolutionary Apps (2014 September 29). ML PlanEx. Retrieved from http://mlplanex.com/revolutionary-apps/

Sadeh, N., Hong, J., Cranor, L., Fette, I., Kelley, P., Prabaker, M., & Rao, J. (2009). Understanding and capturing people's privacy policies in a mobile social networking application. *Personal and Ubiquitous Computing, 13*(6), 401–412.

Salehan, M., & Negahban, A. (2013). Social networking on smartphones: When mobile phones become addictive. *Computers in Human Behavior, 29*(6), 2632–2639.

Schegloff, E.A., Sacks, H., & Weilenmann, A. (2003). "I can't talk now, I'm in a fitting room": Formulating availability and location in mobile-phone conversations. *Environment and Planning A, 35,* 1589–1605.

Seidler, S., & Scope, J. (2014, September 11). Ashkelon teacher: Students exposed naked pictures from my tablet and the school forced me to resign. *Haaretz.* Retrieved from http://www.haaretz.co.il/news/education/.premium-1.2431581.

Smith, E. (2010). iPhone applications & privacy issues: An analysis of application transmission of iPhone unique device identifiers (UDIDs). *URL www. pskl. us/wp/ wp-content/uploads/2010/09/iPhone-Applications-Privacy-Issues. pdf.*

Stern, M. (2014, October 13). 'The snappening' is real: 90,000 private photos and 9,000 hacked snapchat videos leaked online. *The Daily Beast.* Retrieved from http://www.thedailybeast.com/articles/2014/10/13/the-snappening-is-real-90k-private-photos-and-9k-videos-hacked-and-leaked-online.html.

Thompson, D. (2014, June 19). The most popular social network for young people? Texting. *The Atlantic.* Retrieved from http://www.theatlantic.com/technology/archive/2014/06/facebook-texting-teens-instagram-snapchat-most-popular-social-network/373043/.

Tufekci, Z. (2008). Can you see me now? Audience and disclosure regulation in online social network sites. *Bulletin of Science, Technology & Society, 28*(1), 20–36.

Tzuk, N. (2013, June 16). A new record for WhatsApp: 27 billion messages in one day. *Calcalist.* [Hebrew]. Retrieved from http://www.calcalist.co.il/internet/articles/0,7340,L-3605181,00.html.

Waterlow, L. (2014, February 25). Rise of the Brelfie: Breastfeeding selfies are the latest trend for new mums thanks to stars like Miranda Kerr (But is it just 'naked exhibitionism?'). *Daily Mail.* Retrieved from http://www.dailymail.co.uk/femail/article-2968246/Mums-head-head-brelfie-Morning-breastfeeding-selfies-list-parenting-trends-thanks-stars-like-Miranda-Kerr.html.

Watts, L. (2011, February 22). Feature: The Grindr story. *Pink News*. Retrieved from https://www.pinknews.co.uk/2011/02/22/feature-the-grindr-story/.

Wauters, R. (2011, May 10). Done deal! Big deal. Smart deal? Microsoft buys skype for $8.5B in cash. *TechCrunch*. Retrieved from http://techcrunch.com/2011/05/10/microsoft-acquires-skype/.

Williams, A., LaRocca, R., Chang, T., Trinh, N.H., Fava, M., Kvedar, J., & Yeung, (2014). Web-based depression screening and psychiatric consultation for college students: A feasibility and acceptability study. *International Journal of Telemedicine and Applications, 2014*.

Wisniewski, C. (2013, January 29). WhatsApp's privacy investigated by joint Canadian-Dutch probe. *Naked Security*. Retrieved from https://nakedsecurity.sophos.com/2013/01/29/whatsapps-privacy-investigated-by-joint-canadian-dutch-probe/.

Van Den Hoven, J. (2008). Information technology, privacy, and the protection of personal data. In M. J. van den Joven & J. Weckert (Eds.), *Information Technology and Moral Philosophy* (pp. 301–322). Cambridge: Cambridge University Press.

Yaron, O. (2014, August 20). NokNok is taking over the Israeli network, and not everyone is happy about it. *Haaretz Online*. [Hebrew]. Retrieved from http://www.haaretz.co.il/captain/software/.premium-1.2411679.

Chapter 7

Handing Privacy Over

Conclusion

Writing a book on change is not unlike trying to describe a typhoon as it gathers force around you, whipping objects into the air, with steadily increasing wind forces. Privacy is undergoing a comparably stormy period of development. Technology, the Internet, cameras, and common and easily available means of surveillance make privacy protection a complicated difficult challenge; yet the main effect of this transformation is cultural rather than technological.

The current information and communications revolution has changed the social conception of privacy and forged new models of behavior and imitation. The media reflect and shape this new model of privacy, which mirrors the deep changes that have occurred and continue to occur in this field. The media invade the private spheres of all individuals, undermining our privacy, and at the same time, shaping our conception of privacy and the new boundaries of the individual's right to privacy.

The main manifestations of the loss of privacy in television programs, the Internet, and social and mobile media are evident all over the world, including Israel. In this volume several of these manifestations have been explored including how the growing invasion of privacy has gradually obliterated traditional boundaries between public and private spheres. The new media spaces are both private and public, and are more exposed to the public eye than ever before.

Numerous volumes and studies have been published in recent years on various aspects of the loss of privacy and the abuse of privacy as a result of surveillance, collection of personal information, the existence of large databases, the collection of communications data, the security needs and operations of intelligence and security agencies, pervasive cameras, and the commercial activities of companies and corporations that collect, analyze, and use personal information which invade consumers' privacy. These have all created a genuine transformation in the individual's ability to protect his privacy and the confidentiality of his personal information, and they have triggered far-reaching changes that inform the significance, force, validity, and limitations of the right to privacy. These issues have been the topic of investigation by experts in numerous fields including information security, marketing, government and especially the law.

Legalists are concerned that it has become difficult, if not impossible, to protect the right to privacy of citizens and consumers in the information era. The usual response to such concerns is an effort to reinforce the legal right to privacy through supplementary legislation or regulation that would address the more obvious and serious threats to privacy. Such laws, judicial decisions, and regulatory rules attempt to impose prohibitions and restrictions on the parties that collect and use information about us, and obligate them to protect our right to privacy. The European Court even instructed Google to respect the individual's right to be forgotten, and to prevent surfers' access to (correct) information about our history that might be prejudicial to us.

In many cases, such legislation, regulation, and judicial decisions are not truly successful in increasing the substantive right to privacy, inclusive of partial legal engagement and state involvement in these issues, which in itself creates further injury to privacy. It seems that the legal preoccupation with privacy has not yet successfully touched upon the roots or the essence of the current social, moral, and political transformation.

Despite increasing awareness of privacy concerns, as well as increasing worldwide legislation and court decisions concerning privacy rights and protection, many concur that privacy is becoming increasingly compromised and is disappearing. The law is mobilized in an effort to redraw the boundaries of privacy, defining when and under what circumstances information about an individual may be collected, stored, and used; the proper balance between state security and the right to privacy; what a state is permitted to do with the information it collects and stores per citizen; what commercial firms may do with information they obtain from their customers; and the significance and weight of the right to privacy relative to other liberties such as freedom of speech, freedom of occupation, advertising, the right to be forgotten and the public's right to know.

All are important legal issues, but they are merely the external and typically belated manifestations of a deeper fundamental transformation. As always, the law lags behind technological and social change, in an attempt to preserve previous patterns of action and reasoning, with reliance on past precedents—sometimes failing to address the transformation or even grasp its essence altogether.

OUR CHANGING ATTITUDE TO PRIVACY

The preselected option in most interpersonal conversations, even those that take place in public settings, is that interactions are private by default, public through effort. Leaking or recording conversations (for instance) are seen as violations because most people don't assume that their conversations will be publicized if they understand the social situation to be intimate. This is no longer true in the world of social media, which has adopted a "public by default, private through effort" kind of mentality. On a site like Facebook, it is much easier to share with all friends, than to manipulate privacy settings to limit the visibility of the content. "And as a result, many participants make a different calculation than what they would make in an unmediated situation. Rather than asking themselves if the information to be shared is significant enough to be broadly publicized—they question whether it is intimate enough to require special protection" (Boyd, 2014, p. 62). This highlights the change that privacy is undergoing in the digital age and reflects elements of Nissenbaum's theory of contextual integrity, in which she argues that privacy is not binary, that is, something is private or public, but rather depends on the context and the social situation. Therefore, privacy expectations may be seen as relative to the specific social context (Nissenbaum, 2004).

In recent years, the significance and weight that many individuals attribute to privacy have changed enormously, as seen by Boyd's abovementioned statements. What was an important, highly valued principle, commanding respect and protection, has increasingly become an issue of personal exposure alongside growing willingness to invade people's private spaces, almost without restraint.

After all, privacy is a matter of culture, ideology, values, and social behavioral norms. As elaborated elsewhere on the nature of privacy, privacy is a critical, sensitive barometer of an individual's self-identity and place in society. Privacy has different meanings in different societies, varying by geographic location, historical time, social and political culture and technological environment. However, when these parameters undergo tumultuous change, it becomes difficult if not impossible to demarcate the boundaries of privacy or clearly define its nature or significance.

The change in the nature of privacy is the most powerful expression of a deeper social and cultural transformation that human civilization is experiencing as a result of developments in science and communications. This change in privacy is apparently one of the first, but certainly not the final change and it is happening both rapidly and with appalling slowness. The change is sudden, but it is also gradual, and it is reflective of the duality that characterizes our era. We are living in a world without privacy, as many people have stated and at the same time are valiantly fighting for our right to privacy. We promote legislation and government intervention to protect privacy, yet relinquish our privacy without a second thought, in exchange for access to a silly mobile phone game app.

Our changing attitude to privacy is complex and elusive. Overtly, we forgo our privacy; we consent to and actively disclose personal information about ourselves; we tacitly or expressly consent to tools that collect our personal information and track us on all possible media. This volume has offered numerous examples of individuals' desire for exposure, their desire to disclose and share details of their personal lives with others, expose their bodies, their thoughts, their location and emotions, what they eat, consume, and buy.

This is not a mere exchange in which individuals grant their consent or readiness to divulge personal details, using the currency of privacy to obtain other benefits such as discounts, opportunities, focused advertising, personal security, or convenient use of websites or apps. True, this exchange is part of the transformation, and the benefits offered entice people who consciously object to this type of encroachment on their privacy.

An example of such exchange in the field of security is, of course, the wave of legislation that swept the US and the West following 9/11 and the rising tide of terror and crime. States and citizens are willing to use the currency of privacy to obtain some assurance that action is being taken against terror and crime, even accepting the use of methods that increase surveillance and bag searches in public places, inspections at mall entrances, and disclosure of personal information to the state, including biometric data that is used to establish huge databases. Privacy is the price they are willing to pay in exchange for an increase in personal security in this era of rising crime and terror.

Examples from the field of commerce are easy to find since most websites require users to enter their personal information in order to register, including websites that offer a service, convenience or added efficiency. The Israeli GPS app, WAZE, is an excellent example of a program that helps navigation and driving, but in exchange, drivers install a sophisticated tracking program that knows exactly where they are and what they are doing at any given moment, and sells targeted advertising offers accordingly. There are many other websites and apps that take your privacy in exchange for something else—technical assistance, convenience of use, accurate information, personal consultations, or other things that arguably have greater value for the user than the value of the privacy that is relinquished. Indeed, this is an old story. This volume focuses on transformation that is deeper and more significant.

Another, much more significant phenomenon is salient; it is the desire to talk about, share, and make private information public. We typically disguise or tone down our eagerness for disclosure and our readiness to waive our privacy; we refrain from explicitly referring to our actions as a waiver of privacy. We call it sharing, communication, social networks, or an experience. Many of us are eager to participate in reality TV shows, even shows that are explicitly and flagrantly exhibitionist and constitute a serious invasion of privacy, discounting what might have in the past been considered a sweeping waiver of our privacy. Many more maintain social network accounts and pages, write blogs, and regularly upload personal, private and even revealing material that they share with large groups of friends. Moreover, technological developments and digital storage devices make it possible for companies to store mass amounts of data on individuals for an unlimited period of time. Thus, every preferences, move, comment, and like that an individual shares online can be stored indefinitely and used by third-party sources. This "big data" revolution raises questions about privacy as companies like Google know more about us than we remember about ourselves (Mayer-Schönberger, 2011).

Thus, what we are all doing is not merely waiving our privacy. It is much more than that—such actions reflect an eagerness for disclosure, a desire to relinquish control over our personal information. This is a desire that pervades the new pursuit of emotional, factual, and physical exposure which is changing individuals and society.

The Desire to be Observed

Privacy is first and foremost a social norm, and therefore also a given fact in our lives. We use privacy-related situations, described at length in this volume, as a prism through which we offer insights into the emerging social norms in the field of privacy. These are norms that are undergoing a cataclysmic upheaval.

The right to privacy is, however, a legal right, protected by laws and court judgments that grant us rights and power in our relations with others and with our government. Our legal right to privacy gives us control, or more accurately, an illusion of control. This right represents our desire and aspiration to control, limit, and shape others' behaviors toward us. Using the right to privacy, we try to achieve our aspirations of self-realization and prevent others from causing us harm. The right to privacy is based on the idea and the position that we would like to be left alone. In court decisions and scholarly publications following Warren and Brandeis (1890), the modern architects of the right to privacy, this position is known as "the right to be let alone." The legal right to privacy purportedly gives us the power to prevent harassment against us, the power to prohibit others from reading our sealed mail, eavesdropping on our conversations, photographing us in private, or publishing embarrassing images of us. The right to privacy applies to personal and private information such as our medical records or information about our sexual habits as well as to trivial information such as our consumption patterns or Internet-surfing patterns.

The right to privacy is considered one of the rights of individuals in a liberal democratic society, grounded in international conventions and declarations as well as in the constitutions of many countries including the Basic Laws of Israel. All of these documents are expressions of the idea that privacy is an element of an individual's dignity, which is a principle that is protected in conventions and constitutions on human rights. According to the modern approach to privacy, this right is an expression of an individuals' desire to wield maximum control over their own lives and over their autonomous unit, that is, the most important things in their lives that guarantee their identity and freedom. Alan Westin (1967) was the first to define privacy as an individual's right of control.

Today, however, it is evident from a deep, sober study of our society and culture, as we discovered in the process of conducting our studies on privacy in various media and preparing of this manuscript, that the desire to be let alone has been replaced by the new, deeply entrenched and no less powerful desire to be seen, the desire for people to notice the very fact of our existence. This desire may not have entirely replaced the need for privacy, but it has settled squarely alongside it. It is the urge to share, communicate, upload images, perhaps even graphic images, tell your friends and family where you are, what you are doing and eating, and what you are thinking and feeling.

This need and desire has always existed but until now, it seemed that most people contented themselves with sharing information with their partners, family members, and a few friends. Today, technological developments in the media, and of course the penetration of large social networks, the prevalence of smartphones and cameras, the proliferation of surveillance technologies, and their low affordable costs, have suddenly made it possible to pursue an old dream: the dream of becoming famous, the dream of celebrity status, even if fame involves only several dozen or a hundred friends and followers on social media. For many people, access to and the potential of being part of other people's lives highlight the benefits of sharing and the social nature of personage. People receive benefits, sometimes of great value, by becoming members in a community, sharing, uploading images, recipes, tips, news, opinions, thoughts, and emotions. This is not merely the desire to become famous—it is the desire to be present, to be appreciated and loved, and receive "likes" from others.

The facts and data that we present in this volume indicate that many people would like to participate in a reality TV show, be famous, participate in a special experience and reveal their lives completely to a large audience. Ultimately, many more would like to have a large community of friends and affiliates, to whom they regularly report their actions, thoughts, and emotions. Many upload revealing photos of themselves and their families, including their children and their pets, and the food that they eat, and offer their opinions, no matter how unusual or extreme. In the early days of the Internet, we attributed a large part of our sense of freedom and liberation to the fact (true at the time) that the web offered a cloak of anonymity (Branscomb, 1995).

Many people who continue to act and publish information on the Internet still rely on the cloak of anonymity, but an increasing number share, publish, and post personally identifiable, even flagrantly revealing, information on their Facebook, Twitter, or Instagram accounts. The expectation that identifiable social networks would restrain extreme or exhibitionist expressions was proven wrong. In Israel, at least, and apparently in other countries as well, people are expressing extreme opinions on social networks, even when they are completely identified by name and photo. For example, during the War in Gaza in 2014, people expressed extreme and inflamed opinions about the war on their social networks, opening them up to hostile public responses. In extreme cases, statements on Facebook led to the dismissal of employees who had not expressed support for the war against the Hamas enemy. In other cases, people disclosed radical political views openly, clearly identifying themselves in the process. In the chapter on smartphone use, we saw that many people use their smartphones primarily as a means of unconstrained exposure, even if such exposure is partially unconscious.

It seems that many people now realize their freedom and their dignity by using the public sphere to expose and disclose, and seek the support and admiration of a broad or focused target audience. The desire to be left alone has been replaced by the fear of being left alone, being alone, being observed by no one, with no one noticing or caring. Perhaps in the future the right to be left alone—the right to privacy—will be supplanted by a new legal right: the right of not being alone, the right to share and participate.

The Right to Not Be Alone

Alongside the desire for control and privacy, a new, deeper and no less significant aspiration has emerged: the desire to be observed, the desire not to be alone. An individual realizes his autonomy not only in isolation, in the privacy of his home and castle, but through relationships with others. Today's modern media and available technologies allow us to easily share with the world, with our friends both near and distant, what was in the past private and personal. The same deep desire for control, for self-identity, for realization of our autonomy as individuals, the desire that triggered the right to privacy, has in recent years prompted and fanned the desire to share, to elicit comments and responses, to be seen, and to be an object of attention in the public sphere. In effect, the boundary between the private and public sphere has become obliterated entirely. What we once hoped to receive at home, we now would also like to receive outside the home, from a larger audience.

As elaborated, young people and specifically teenage girls no longer write journal entries that are kept under lock and key in a desk drawer—they post their entries as blogs on the Internet, expressing their desire to be famous, to be seen and to be present, even if they are doing so under the cover of partial anonymity. Their desire is to be present and attract responses; otherwise they have no sense of truly existing. To develop their self-identity, they need the mirrors held up by their audiences, readers and others.

People are becoming more preoccupied with the question of how to cause others to read their personal musings and view the images and photos they upload, than with the question of how to prevent them from doing so. More people are trying to encourage others to photograph them and upload their photos to the Internet, than to prevent others from capturing them on film. People are doing everything possible to shout out their messages, and are less concerned about being objects of surveillance, or being bugged, overheard, or followed as the analysis of smartphone behavior in the public sphere has demonstrated.

People make entirely private and intimate use of their phones when—and perhaps primarily because—they are in public spaces. Selfies are the pure expression of our personal, intimate and touching use of the camera to take our own photos, a use that is a distillation of narcissism and privacy, but we do so openly in the public sphere, with the aim of distributing the photo to a growing number of friends.

A broad look at our private and public spaces indicates that the last remaining private sphere is that very same smartphone we carry with us everywhere. It contains our deepest secrets, the details of our identity and autonomy. Without it, we are lost. The information contained in our smartphones is vast and absolutely personal, but, most importantly, the smartphone is our means of communication whose main and most significant purpose is to connect us to the world. We use our privacy so that we are not alone: The key value is **connectivity**. We have a stronger need to be connected, to talk, to photograph, to share, and to be visible and present. All these actions effectively represent privacy waived in order to realize individual dignity and autonomy. The inversion is complete: No longer is ours a desire for privacy but rather an aspiration and desire to become part of a group, part of a network, to be together, to be seen and heard, a desire not to be left alone.

In fact, in today's modern society a person's supreme right is the right to be connected. The digital divide separates those who have a connection—and therefore have value—to the pitiful others who remain on the sideline, with no Internet connection nor smartphone nor ability to communicate, receive, and transmit messages about the world and about themselves. For many people, an individual's main value lies in the number of his friends and followers on Facebook, Twitter, and Instagram. The fame, publicity, and ability to reach many others are what determines an individual's identity and value. This is the new individual dignity. The distinction between private and public has imploded altogether.

Public Sphere and Private Sphere

The distinction between public and private is one of the foundations of human society. The dichotomy between the two has cardinal significance for a long list of issues. The collapse of this distinction, or its extensive obliteration, is effectively the basis of the transformation of privacy. The implications of this collapse far exceed the issue of privacy and its representation in the various media. The distinction between private and public still has enormous significance in individuals' everyday lives, but the fundamental difference in the past, between private property and homes, and the street or public park, or the differences between private and public law are disappearing. Feminism has denounced this distinction in its struggle against male domination of women based on what happens in "private" spheres. Homosexuals have pointed out that the "public space" is a heterosexual space, relegating others to the "private" sphere. Work performed at home; employers' intrusion into their employees' lives at all hours of the day, using media; nannycams—these and many others exemplify the complete obliteration of the distinction between public and private. We are never alone, and there is hardly any space that is free from intervention by public social norms. Children's rights, which are universally valid, have supplanted parents' right to privacy or parents' right to raise their children as they see fit in their own homes. The panopticon, conceived by Bentham and invoked (analyzed?) by Foucault—a prison structured to ensure that prisoners never know whether or not they are being observed by their guard—has become our reality, in which we conduct ourselves as if subject to incessant observation. Big Brother reality shows, which have been discussed extensively, represent the extreme culmination of the collapse of the distinction between the ostensibly private home and the public space. In this popular reality show, participants celebrate the fact that they are constantly being observed by the audience, as they draw enjoyment and satisfaction from the situation.

The expectation that participants' awareness of being monitored would cause them to restrain their conduct and limit their self-exposure, self-restricting their freedom of action, falls apart in the world of the Big Brother shows, where participants, despite their being in a public space and observed by 40% of the country's television audience, act in a completely unrestricted and uncontrolled manner, revealing facts, bodies, and emotions, to the point of falling in love and willingly engaging in intercourse on the show. As described in the chapter on the show, the sixth season of Big Brother in

Israel brought such exposure to a fascinating peak, where one of the participants, who knew that everything was being filmed and revealed, "in private"
manipulated the two young women who had fallen in love with him, and told
each of them "privately" that he loved them. Producers' instruction to the
participants to "act appropriately" during live broadcasts is especially ironic
in view of the collapsed distinction between public and private. Participants
who are supposedly in a private home are required to act according to public
norms only during live broadcasts, and such instructions supposedly remove
them from the private to the public sphere.

They are, in any case, always in the public sphere, and their conduct
always conforms to the norms of exposure. What is fascinating is that today,
the norm of exposure—when one knows that the entire public is watching
you—is the norm of privacy. Act normally, be yourself, act as if you are in
your private space: You will gain popularity only when you act naturally and
authentically in public, as if you are in the privacy of your own home.

This is also the imperative of social networks: Show us yourselves and
your true, intimate, personal details, but reveal them to everyone, everywhere, at all times.

The fact that we photograph ourselves incessantly, even in restricted
places or places that were considered private in the past, and upload these
photos to an unrestricted social network, which is a pure example of a public
space, and the fact that we use our very private mobile phones especially
when we are in public spaces have obliterated the distinction even further.
The collapsed boundary between public and private has inevitably led to a
decline in the right to privacy, which is defined in many countries including
the US and Israel as the right that protects an individual's reasonable expectations of privacy. What is a reasonable expectation of privacy in a world
devoid of private space? Apparently no such expectations can survive if we
know, or should know, that we are always being followed, under surveillance, and that our GPS system "knows" exactly where we are and probably
what we are doing.

A compelling physical indication of the dissipating private sphere is
the disappearance of public telephone booths on city streets. Once upon a
time, there were closed booths that contained a telephone for public use; it
was taken for granted that individuals who wanted to conduct a telephone
conversation required privacy and a closed, personal space. The individual
would enter the booth and close the door behind her. Today, in the era of
the mobile smartphone, such a space is neither necessary nor conceivable.
Everyone is used to overhearing other people's telephone calls, which can be
very personal, at all times. What once may have been embarrassing has now
become the norm: we ignore these conversations and forget their contents
immediately.

Today we understand that even our most private and personal space is usually subject to surveillance, photography, and intrusion. Our private images may be exposed by hackers. Our databases are only slightly protected, as are our credit information, medical records, and whatever information we retain in digital form. Past concerns over invasion of our private space have been replaced by new concerns regarding the potential intrusion into our private thoughts, dreams, and what goes on in our brain, the stuff that provides fertile ground for innovative research as well as for popular culture and for films. Our thoughts are the only private space remaining private, and they too can be expected to be uncovered in the future.

Crises and Loss of Control

Crises involving a loss of privacy and a loss of control over information have become an important commonplace phenomenon in the information era. Lost control over private information and leaks of sensitive confidential information from secured databases still evoke anger and cause serious harm to the victims. On the face of it, this phenomenon signals that the desire for privacy remains strong and powerful, and the need to protect the right to privacy still exists. Such crises call for a thorough analysis and discussion: How is it possible that, in a world devoid of privacy, expectations of privacy and anger at failures to protect privacy are so common? Here, we would like to focus on two important features or elements of such crises; both features have a lot to teach us about contemporary trends concerning privacy norms and the right to privacy.

One important question is, when does such a crisis occur, or what is it in the accepted expectation of privacy that evokes such objections, anger and powerful public and legal responses when violated? The crisis and the fierce response that it sparks reinforce the feeling that some critical boundary has indeed been breached and that privacy has been violated in an unreasonable, damaging manner. The damage is horrific, and the victims are shell-shocked. It is important to stop at this point and try to understand the nature of the damage and the intensity of the emotions that emerge even in a world of greatly diminished privacy.

The second feature is the reverse effect: the crisis diminishes privacy further. After all, every media crisis relating to infringements of our right to privacy proves to everyone, as individuals and as a society, that no effective technological, economic, social or legal means to prevent such privacy violations exist. In this manner, the crisis becomes one of many elements that inform the contemporary norms of privacy. We all understand that the right to privacy is about protecting our reasonable expectations of privacy, but is it reasonable for such expectations to persist, in view of the reality of repeated violations of privacy? Clearly, by affecting everyone's awareness that all existing information is ultimately destined to be exposed, such incidents involving privacy violations, information leaks, disclosures, and the publication of personal or sensitive private information reduce our reasonable expectations of privacy, rendering them illogical and unrealistic.

A significant example of such a crisis occurred in September 2014 when dozens and perhaps hundreds of nude photos of film stars, actresses, models, and performers including Jennifer Lawrence and Kate Upton were downloaded, from what were considered secure Apple servers, and posted on social networks—primarily on Twitter (see Newsweek report). News of the penetration of Apple's iCloud and publication of the intimate nude photos led to sharp responses by the victims and by government agencies, calling the act a "flagrant violation of privacy" and triggering a public debate on whether the celebrities themselves were in some way responsible, having photographed themselves in the nude and saved the photos in the Cloud. Others believed that since these stars had already appeared fully or partially nude in the media, in films, or in magazines, the violation of their privacy was not so grave a matter, and there was no actual difference between these secret pictures and other pictures that were available on the Internet by a simple search. What is interesting about this incident is that it exposed the powerful desire for control, which has largely replaced the need for privacy. The affair exposed and highlighted the economic interests related to privacy, transforming privacy into property or a consumer good: The photos were clearly worth large sums of money to the celebrities.

On the one hand, this crisis made it clear to all models, stars, and in fact to all individuals, that their intimate photos in the cloud might wind up in the public sphere and be disseminated on Twitter. On the other hand, the crisis highlighted the gap between victims' expectations of privacy and the situation as it really is. The celebrities had innocently believed that these photos could be prevented from reaching the public.

We argue that this expectation—that the photos would remain outside the public domain—is more about a desire for control and concern about the economic value of proprietary rights to the photos than about embarrassment or a genuine fear that the exposure would violate one's privacy and dignity. Legalists have already pointed to the connection between justifying privacy as a need for control, and the conception of privacy as property. Lawrence Lessig (2006), for example, believes that privacy should be considered property that can be sold and purchased, at values set by its owners. He believes that this would reinforce privacy and its status (Lessig, 2006).

Clearly the conception of privacy as property implies that the information will be sold on the market, and contradicts the fundamental conception of human dignity. It seems that today, the victims themselves focus on the legal offense perpetrated against them, the fact that their legal rights were violated, their property was stolen, and they incurred significant economic damage, even more strongly, or perhaps independently of the original and deeper sense of protection of privacy which safeguards individual autonomy and dignity against the shame and anguish caused by exposure.

The paradox is that the nature of privacy should be based on social norms and on the expectation of privacy, rather than on legal defenses. What we are trying to say is that in some of the lawsuits or cases of loss of privacy, the damage incurred by the victims concerns their pockets or the economic potential represented by their personal information, more than it concerns genuine damage to their dignity or autonomy.

The growing gap between privacy as a human value and privacy as property and a legal right of control has emerged recently, increasingly separating what the public considers a legal right from empirical reality. As always, in this case too, the law lags behind social and technological developments and behind the media that shape social norms. Major crises, such as the incident involving the stolen celebrity photos (Issac, 2014), highlight this gap between expectations, based on broad legal protection of the right to privacy, and the reality created by the media and technology, or in other words, the reality of social norms. Celebrities expect legal protection and therefore feel that they have incurred genuine damage by a violation of their legal right. There is no doubt in this case that a legal right has been violated. The issue here is that it is doubtful whether any genuine harm was caused to the social norms of privacy or to the values that the right to privacy protects. It is similarly doubtful whether stars who make a living from their exposed images honestly feel a sense of shame, anguish, pain, or injury to their dignity as a result of the publication of their photos without their permission. The issue here may be one of harm and injury, and may even be deserving of legal protection, but it is doubtful whether it is privacy that was violated.

The analysis of the way we expose ourselves on the various media platforms indicates that we seek exposure on a daily basis. We are conscious of and use these media daily, incessantly photographing ourselves and making these images public. This is certainly true of film stars, performers, and models. The social norm that technology and the media have created is the norm of exposure. The media and technology have habituated us to the availability of photos of partially and even fully nude celebrities. As a result, anyone who distributes such photos does not consider himself to be causing others harm or violating their individual dignity.

The injury caused by illegal publication is harm to a person's reputation: This is economic harm caused to the right to publication, and of course, a loss of control. As we learn from major privacy crises, despite our need and desire for exposure, and although we live in a technological reality in which almost any information about us will find its way to publication, we still want to be paid every time information about us is published; we still want to retain control over everything published about us; we want to control privacy as our property, and we still get angry when other people profit from the exposure of our information at our expense. The question is whether these are legitimate desires that society and the law should validate. Today's media- and technology-shaped norm is different, and the celebrities' use of patterns of privacy rooted in the past may arguably be considered hypocritical, even though they are reflected in the law.

As a society, we should understand that the law will not indefinitely provide excessive protection for norms that are no longer acceptable, and will not grant excessive powers to prohibit or prevent publication of information, even if such prohibitions are conventional practice. Preventing the use and dissemination of the information, knowledge, and data needed for the public interest is not only an abuse of this right and a violation of the freedom of expression, the public's right to know, and the freedom of occupation—it is also hypocrisy. In the field of privacy, social norms should shape legal rules and not vice versa.

The Need for Privacy

Changes in the concept of privacy, increasing technological options, and growing individual desires for self-expression, self-exposure, and publication of personal information and opinions on anything and everything in the world, have also heightened many people's needs and desires to use anonymity when expressing themselves or operating on media platforms. As we have seen in various chapters, anonymity constitutes a kind of interim space between full, absolute exposure and lack of privacy on the one hand, and a state of withdrawal, secrecy, non response, isolation, and complete privacy, on the other. Anonymity allows one to detach actions from actors, and provides freedom of action to such actors who want to act but are apprehensive about the implications and outcomes of their actions; actors who would like to perform a specific act but prefer to have no one know that it was them.

People who are truly concerned about their privacy and isolate themselves from the world are not the people who refrain from publishing their work or opinions anonymously, refrain from donating semen, are not whistle-blowers, do not give money to charity anonymously, are not active on meeting websites and do not write heated talkbacks using a pseudonym.

Anonymity is itself an elusive concept. We should distinguish between complete anonymity—or a situation in which it is impossible to identify or trace a message to its source, or attribute it to a specific, identifiable person—and the state of pseudonimity, in which the individual adopts a name she uses to operate on the media, and build an independent reputation, audience, and readership, effectively constructing a virtual persona and identity that exists alongside the identifiable individual identity.

Internet space has become a broad arena of anonymous activity, which includes teenage blogging, Wikipedia, Second Life, meeting websites, and talkbacks; Yet despite the availability of anonymity and pseudonimity options, people continue to march toward full exposure. We believe that this is a significant and interesting interim stage, which plays an important role in culture and society, facilitating a gradual transition from the world of privacy to the world of exposure and an absence of solitude.

Anonymity allows one to play with exposure, teasing its flames and its underlying dangers, without leaping into the fire. Anonymity gives one the frequently illusory sense of being unreachable, the sense that personal identity is undisclosable and no sensitive information, publication or action can be traced back to her. And yet, publication grants one a sense of significance and presence; in many cases, comments provide support, acceptance, and even love. From their anonymous presence in the public sphere and the responses they receive there, people gain the sense that they are not alone.

In most cases, anonymity implies the non-identification of an individual in a group. We may know that the individual belongs to a certain group—an age group, a geographic area, a group of origin or users of a specific medium, or a specific category of consumers. Sometimes this may be a group of participants in a study or a group of sources for a news item. In any case, the core of anonymity is, then, the absence of a traceable connection between an identified individual and an identified act. In such cases, the action is overt— publication of an opinion, a work of art, disclosure of information, or a review of an academic paper—but the person who performed the act is not identified.

Anonymity remains an important and prevalent social, political and legal practice in many contexts of our lives. The numerous situations in which society uses the tool of anonymity include anonymous charitable donation giving, academic reviewing, anonymous tenders, medical lab tests, addict support groups, the use of cash, safeguarding the identity of adopted children, secret ballots, whistle-blowing, reporter's privilege, publication of anonymous works of art or literature, talkbacks or Internet blogs, and anonymous website surfing.

Anonymity makes a tangible contribution to people's freedom of expression and their ability to express themselves, to expose and leak information to the press, and to serve the public's right to know. In US law, the right to anonymity is part of the constitutional right of freedom of speech, which is protected under the First Amendment. In Israel, some view anonymity as an integral part of the right to privacy. In our context, anonymity and pseudonimity constitute an important stage in the gradual transformation of the concept of privacy, and their significance increases the more privacy collapses and disappears. In a world where tracking personal information is so easy, in a world of such strong desires and needs for exposure, anonymity is an oasis— a stepping stone. The information exists, the action is known, but the actor's identity as a direct connection tying to the act is not always apparent.

The right to anonymity can generally replace the right to privacy: It can provide for most of the needs that we generally seek in the right to privacy. Most people are not concerned by the fact that extensive information about them is being collected, as long as none of the information is directly linked to them. Data collection is merely the aggregation of personal information, typical of the majority of online commercial and marketing operations that grant anonymity to consumers while they use the collected data to increase customer service and efficiency and to facilitate increasingly targeted advertising.

In a world of anonymity, this state is clearly the exception. The rule is exposure and identity and the exception is anonymity. In this normative reality, the privilege of anonymity also has its limits—that is, there are moments of disclosure, of removing masks or of exposure (Solove, 2007). Thinking in terms of partial anonymity can close the distance between a reality dominated by an absence of privacy on the one hand, and the ubiquitous desire to control the amount, the nature and the location of exposure.

THE CASE OF ISRAEL

The Israeli context is studied here as a model of phenomena that are now, or expected to be worldwide in the future. Israel is an example of a society that was an early adopter of communications technologies and whose conceptions of privacy have undergone rapid transformation. The collectivist roots of Israeli society established a collaborative society in which privacy originally had little value; as individualism increased, privacy became a priority. Once almost a vulgarism, at the end of the twentieth century privacy became an important, and even constitutional right. Anonymity, which is virtually impossible in a small, crowded country where many people know others personally, expanded as the country's population grew from 600,000 at independence to eight million plus today.

Israel is an especially interesting test case. Israeli society is not only characterized by rapid adoption of communications technologies, but also by an extremely powerful drive to obliterate the boundaries separating the public and the private, and a desire for a sense of overall intimacy and togetherness.

In his book "The Code of Israeliness," Gad Yair (2011), who heads the Department of Sociology and Anthropology at the Hebrew University of

Jerusalem, lists the ten commandments of Israeli society. Three of the ten commandments concern privacy. One refers to the use of the public sphere as if it were a private sphere. Yair states that "[i]t is not clear whether Israelis understand the concept of the public sphere" and he quotes someone as saying, "No matter where you are in the world, you act as if you're at home." Another principle of Israeliness is collectivism and inquisitiveness, the tendency of Israelis to intervene in the private business of other Israelis, including complete strangers. Society is characterized by a high level of collaboration, a strong sense of familial affiliation, and the tendency to ask and accept assistance from strangers. The third code concerns privacy, intimacy among strangers, and the ease of contact with others. Israelis will conduct intimate and revealing conversations with other Israelis who are strangers, as if they were close friends or family members. Discussing this type of immediate intimacy, Yair determines, "Strangers here feel as if we are invading their private spaces, that within minutes we will discuss intimate matters that they wouldn't ordinarily discuss with someone they've known for less than a year."

In this book, we illustrate how Israeli society has reverted to its collectivist roots as new technologies and the desire to belong to a "community" have increased. The new privacy, which was reinstated by virtue of technological developments, created an interesting situation in which privacy is not only cast as the opposite of publicness, but it is also fragmented into various facets of privacy: personal privacy, family privacy and privacy of friends, among others. Technology and communications allow Israeliness to reach full, emphatic expression in all media, erasing those spaces that are restrictive, closed or private.

We now have new circles of privacy—friends, family, work—and the boundaries separating these circles have become blurred as one circle spills over to another. In itself, spillover implies a loss of privacy. The desire to protect privacy as it existed in the past has almost disappeared, and today we face a new interpretation of privacy.

THE ANONYMITY OF PRIVACY

The concept of privacy has been discussed in detail, type by type. For the first time here, we have made a distinction between the exposure of personal factual information, physical information, and emotional exposure and the significance of the loss of privacy in each dimension. This is the first typology of its kind, as it touches upon the ways in which we choose to expose ourselves. If privacy is a matter of consent, a matter of social norms, of culture, time, and place—then understanding the meaning of privacy is possible only through the study and understanding of the different ways we expose ourselves, shedding our masks and the guise of privacy and secrecy that envelopes us. Previous efforts to classify privacy were conducted mainly from an external perspective looking inward, that is, they were classifications of external actions that violate privacy. For example, the most comprehensive classification known was proposed by Solove (2008), who suggested 16 situations of privacy violations, divided into four types of privacy invasions.

The first four types are information collection, information processing, information dissemination and invasions into a person's life and intervention in his decisions. This is an important and fascinating division, but it fails to capture the ways in which people willingly relinquish their privacy. Privacy research has always concerned violations of rights, its threat and harm to individuals, which has therefore increasingly supported reinforcing the legal right, disregarding the much more significant developments of recent years: the process of exposure. The detailed study of the manner in which rights are violated when people's information is collected, processed, and disseminated, disregards the more commonplace cases in which people willingly grant access to their information, and permit—perhaps even facilitate—its collection, processing, and dissemination.

Our study uncovers the ways we are exposed—on television, on reality shows, on the Internet, on social networks, through the blogs we post, through our everyday use of our smartphones and their apps. It notes that it is the willingness and even desire to share information that specifically fuels the technologies of information collection, processing and dissemination.

Of course, it is not our intention to understate the dangers posed by intrusive collection of personal information, illicit use of such information, its exploitation, and the potential harm caused to individuals, even when the source of such dangers is the individual's own consent and self-exposure. In many cases, we can identify the individual's confusion, lack of awareness of the exposure implicit inactions, desire to safeguard control and secrets, and at same time, desire to use new technologies and benefit from the convenience and security that they offer. The psychological dimension of the need and desire for privacy remains evident in the public sphere as well as in the media, and is beyond the scope of this book. Many people and different personality types still cling to and yearn for privacy, and are concerned by any potential loss of privacy.

THE TRANSITION FROM PRIVACY TO THE DESIRE NOT TO BE LEFT ALONE

Thus, throughout this book (and for all the various media) concerns of privacy have been replaced by the fear of being alone, unconnected, devoid of ties or comments. After all, people have always wanted to be loved, to be surrounded by friends, to be popular; so what has changed? Why were we so concerned about privacy one hundred years ago whereas our contemporary concerns have shifted to a completely different focus? The shift is deep, and touches upon far-reaching changes in culture, society and interpersonal relations. The explanation for the profound change we have undergone which essentially changes the nature of privacy, concerns our needs as human beings, including, first and foremost, the need to belong, to be loved and popular, and the different methods for satisfying these needs. We are not psychologists, and this book mainly focuses on changes in society, media, and the social and legal norms that accompany these changes, but ultimately, the explanation for these changes does not lie solely with technology but also in the relationship between technology, the media, culture, and society.

When seeking the background and reasons for people's need for privacy, we are touching upon the roots of the transformation itself. We believe that in the past, in the golden age of the right to privacy, people's strong desire for privacy stemmed from these same human needs: the need to belong and be loved and popular within society. In that era, people were seriously concerned that if they revealed the truth about their private lives, they would be subject to criticism, condemnation and even ostracization. Exposing your body, the details of a serious medical condition, or your sexual habits or preferences in public could lead to condemnation and loss of social status. Shame dominated that era, and people needed privacy as they needed air to breathe. Privacy was critical in a society based on hypocrisy, manners, rigid social norms, hierarchy, repression and intolerance of difference. You were advised to hide your real life and your private thoughts and cover them in a shield of privacy to be realized only in private spaces.

In other words, privacy is designed to protect the fabric of human relations in a society that maintains distinct social norms in the public and private spheres; in a society unable to accept the other, the exception, or the individual suffering from a handicap or disease. It is very important for such people to be able to protect the confidentiality of such personal and medical information, and their efforts to maintain such secrecy should be supported by a legal right to privacy that allows them to do so. In Israel, 15 years ago, Ofra Haza, a celebrated singer who had contracted AIDS, adamantly refused to be hospitalized because it would have exposed the terrible secret of disease. Ofra Haza died of AIDS, but in fact she died of shame. Had she not been ashamed of her condition and admitted herself to a hospital, chances are that she would have recovered.

Today, in our open free society, which accepts the fact that people have different sexual proclivities, challenges, medical conditions, and strange personal thoughts or unusual habits, keeping a secret no longer has such significance. In a liberal society that advocates humanism, liberalism and acceptance of individual diversity, there is no longer any true need to hide or be ashamed. There is no fear that personal private information, the disclosure of facts, body parts or strong emotions, will prompt censure or isolation. Perhaps the opposite is even true. The intensity of exposure in the media is the result of our understanding that even complete personal exposure cannot necessarily cause harm or lead to isolation, but rather may accomplish the opposite by generating support, popularity and identification. The paradigm has inverted itself. Now the exposure of weakness, limitations, needs and emotions is what creates a sense of affinity, support and social connection.

We have always wanted to be popular and a part of society, and to be in tune with its dominant norms and values. In the past, we achieved these desires by protecting our privacy. People needed to show one side to the people closest to them at home and another side in the public sphere. Today, as shown in this book, the media are pointing to a different route. To connect to others and fit it, we now shed our cloaks and allow others to observe us, to learn about us and to follow us, almost with no restriction. In this view, currently, one becomes part of society as a whole and gains recognition and love. Of course, the process is long and complicated and it is also dependent on culture, time, and place.

FACING THE FUTURE

In this book, the discussion of the changing significance of privacy has been extended and has displayed that the accelerated transformation of privacy that has occurred in Israel may be a predictive model for similar changes elsewhere in the world. We believe that the change in the concept of privacy is not merely a change for the worse, it is also a change for the better. Exposure, transparency, acceptance of diversity, a sense of support and community—all of these can compensate for the loss of control and autonomy entailed in the loss of privacy as we once knew it.

Our new world is a world devoid of traditional conceptions of privacy—we must become accustomed to these changes and enjoy the advantages

REFERENCES

Boyd, D. (2014). *It's complicated: The social lives of networked teens*. New Haven, CT: Yale University Press.

Branscomb A.W. (1995). Anonymity, autonomy and accountability: Challenges to the first amendment in cyberspace. *Yale Law Journal, 104*(7), 1639–1679.

Isaac, M. (2014, September 2). Nude photos of Jennifer Lawrence are latest front in online privacy debate. *NY Times*. Retrieved from http://www.nytimes.com/2014/09/03/technology/trove-of-nude-photos-sparks-debate-over-online-behavior.html?_r=0.

Grant, M. (2014, September 2). Hundreds of intimate celebrity pictures leaked online following alleged iCloud breach. Retrieved from http://www.newsweek.com/hundreds-intimate-celebrity-pictures-leaked-online-following-suspected-icloud-267851.

Lessig, L. (2006). *Code version* 2.0. New York: Basic Books.

Nissenbaum, H. (2004). Privacy as contextual integrity. *Washington Law Review, 79*(1), 119–157.

Mayer-Schönberger, V. (2011). *Delete: The virtue of forgetting in the digital age.* Woodstock, Oxfordshire, UK: Princeton University Press.

Warren, S., & Brandeis, L. (1890). The right to privacy. *Harvard Business Review*, 193.

Solove, D. (2007). *The future of reputation: Gossip, rumor, and privacy on the internet.* New Haven: Yale University Press.

Solove, D. (2008). *Understanding privacy.* Boston: Harvard University Press.

Westin, A. (1967). *Privacy and freedom.* New York: Athenuem Books.

Yair G. (2011). *The code of Israeliness: The ten commandments for the 21ˢᵗ century.* Jerusalem: Keter Books.

Index

About the Authors

Yuval Karniel is a senior lecturer at the Sammy Ofer School of Communications at the Interdisciplinary Center (IDC) Herzliya where he gives courses on Media Policy, Ethics and Law in the Media, Media and Power, and Crisis Management and is the Co-Chair of IDC's Content Hub. He is the author of "Breach of Trust in Corporations" (2001) and "The Laws of the Commercial Media" (2003). He is also the Founder of the Israeli Movement for Freedom of Information.

Karniel's areas of expertise are media and the law, copyright, new media, telecommunications, privacy, ethics, IP and regulation. He was the Chairman of the Ethics Committee for the Israeli Broadcasting Authority and the Chairman of the Science and Technology Committee for the Israeli Bar Association. Previously, he served as the first General Counsel of Israel's Commercial TV and Radio Authority, and was a member of the Board of Directors of Bezeq—Israel's leading communications company.

Karniel is an honors graduate of the Hebrew University in Jerusalem and holds a Master in International Law from The American University in Washington DC. He received his doctorate (LL.D) at Hebrew University Law School in 1997.

Amit Lavie-Dinur is Vice Dean and Head of Content, Marketing and Political Specializations at the Sammy Ofer School of Communications at the Interdisciplinary Center (IDC) Herzliya, Israel. She is a senior lecture of Media, Culture and Communication and gives courses in theory of communication, propaganda in television and new media and popular texts.

Lavie-Dinur holds a Master Degree from New York University (NYU) and a Doctorate (Phd.) from Hebrew University in Jerusalem, Israel. She has published numerous articles on a variety of subjects in professional journals on International communication, cultural aspects of advertising, privacy and reality TV. She was an executive member of the Israel Film Council and served as a selector for the New Israel Foundation for Cinema and TV. Today she is a council member at the Second Authority for Television & Radio.

CPSIA information can be obtained at www.ICGtesting.com
Printed in the USA
BVOW08*0931281115

428222BV00003B/3/P